Philadelphia Phillies 2019

A Baseball Companion

Edited by Patrick Dubuque, Aaron Gleeman and Bret Sayre

Baseball Prospectus

Craig Brown and Dave Pease, Consultant Editors
Rob McQuown and Harry Pavlidis, Statistics Editors

Copyright © 2019 by DIY Baseball, LLC.
All rights reserved

This book or any part thereof may not be reproduced or transmitted in any form or by any means, electronic or mechanical, including photocopying, recording, or by any information storage and retrieval system, without permission in writing from the publisher.

Limit of Liability/Disclaimer of Warranty: While the publisher and the author have used their best efforts in preparing this book, they make no representations or warranties with respect to the accuracy or completeness of the contents of this book and specifically disclaim any implied warranties of merchantability or fitness for a particular purpose. No warranty may be created or extended by sales representatives or written sales materials. The advice and strategies contained herein may not be suitable for your situation. You should consult with a professional where appropriate. Neither the publisher nor the author shall be liable for any loss of profit or any other commercial damages, including but not limited to special, incidental, consequential, or other damages.

Library of Congress Cataloging-in-Publication Data:
paperback
ISBN-13: 978-1-949332-48-3

Project Credits
Cover Design: Kathleen Dyson
Interior Design and Production: Jeff Pease, Dave Pease
Layout: Jeff Pease, Dave Pease

Baseball icon courtesy of Uberux, from https://www.shareicon.net/author/uberux

Ballpark diagram courtesy of Lou Spirito/THIRTY81 Project, https://thirty81project.com/

Manufactured in the United States of America
10 9 8 7 6 5 4 3 2 1

Table of Contents

Foreword v
   Rob Mains

Statistical Introduction vii

Part 1: Team Analysis

Table for Two: Previewing the 2019 Philadelphia Phillies 3
   Paul Boyé and Justin Klugh

Performance Graphs 9

2018 Team Performance 10

2019 Team Projections 11

Team Personnel 12

Citizens Bank Park Stats 13

Phillies Team Analysis 15

Part 2: Player Analysis

Phillies Player Analysis 22

Phillies Prospects 103

Part 3: Featured Articles

The Hole in The Shift is Fixing Itself 117
   Russell Carleton

The State of the Quality Start 121
   Rob Mains

Heads-Up Hacking—The First Pitch 127
   Matthew Trueblood

A Hymn for the Index Stat 133
   Patrick Dubuque

Index of Names 137

Foreword

Rob Mains

Welcome to this companion of the 2019 Philadelphia Phillies. We at Baseball Prospectus are excited to provide this analysis of the Phillies.

Our website, Baseball Prospectus, is a leader in delivering high-quality commentary and data to baseball fans everywhere. To some, those words—commentary and data—appear mutually exclusive. There are people out there who believe that traditional analysis and advanced analytics must run on different paths. But the simplistic narrative of stats vs. traditionalists just isn't true. Every team's analytics department interacts with scouting, development, and major league operations with a common goal: Delivering a championship. New technologies, like radar tracking of pitch speeds and movement, enable talent evaluators to focus on qualitative aspects of pitching like mechanics and pitch sequencing. In-game strategies like infield shifts, based on batters' hit tendencies, help turn balls in play into outs. Hitters use information to adjust their swings to maximize run production.

All these numbers can seem, at best, intimidating, and at worst, counterproductive to the casual fan. Even as technology and analysis have embedded themselves deeply into the way teams run, it can often feel like statistics create a displacement between the viewer and the sport, breaking them out of the action. And yet every fan incorporates the numbers to some degree; stats like batting average and earned run average, so fundamental to how we talk about performance, are actually complicated formulas. They don't bother people because those formulas have become second nature, as easy to translate as the action on the field.

Along the way, new statistics have entered baseball's lexicon. You'll see some of them, like on-base percentage (which measures a batter's ability to get on base via walk, hit batter, or hit), OPS (on-base plus slugging), and average exit velocity (the speed of balls off a hitter's bat) on broadcasts. Others, like DRC+, might well be new to you. Some of them have been well-defined to the public, others haven't. That lack of context has created ambiguity. Fans know that a ball hit 100 mph is scorched, but does that mean extra bases? (Not if it's hit on the ground or high in the air it doesn't.)

For those who are amenable to them, the new statistics can increase the enjoyment and understanding of the game. They can help fans identify when a pitcher is tiring, when a stolen base or a bunt attempt makes sense (and, more often, when it doesn't), or how a team's lineup might be constructed. Websites like Baseball Prospectus add to that understanding by weaving metrics into the narrative of the game. That's the goal of this publication: to take some of the newer, more complicated statistics and make them as intuitive as the ones on the back of old baseball cards.

But you don't need to love analytics to love baseball. The fans at BP who worked together to write this guide are captivated first and foremost by the game itself. We're drawn to Aaron Judge's power, Francisco Lindor's glove, Billy Hamilton's speed and Patrick Corbin's slider and don't need numbers to tell us why they're so mesmerizing. The underlying statistics provide depth to the game that we all love.

We hope you'll find that this guide helps you better understand the Phillies. Our analysts have studied the team's major league personnel and its minor league affiliates to identify their strengths and weaknesses, both the obvious ones and those that only a careful dissection of players' performances—yes, including the data—can reveal. You don't need us to tell you who was good and who wasn't in 2018, but our models and writers can help you project how each player is going to perform this year and beyond, and appreciate the greatness of each new game as it unfolds. As in the sport itself, the human and analytic components combine to generate a deeper overall understanding.

Think back to the first time you saw a baseball game on a high-definition TV. You'd grown familiar with how the game looked and felt on a picture tube. But new TV allowed you to see details that you'd never seen before. That's how advanced statistics work. The game itself is why you're here and why you're buying this. (And, for that matter, why we wrote it.) The statistical measures provide the sharper focus, the detail, the depth of knowledge that you didn't have before, generating an overall superior picture. Enjoy the view.

—*Rob Mains is an author of Baseball Prospectus.*

Statistical Introduction

Sports are, fundamentally, a blend of athletic endeavor and storytelling. Baseball, like any other sport, tells its stories in so many ways: in the arc of a game from the stands or a season from the box scores, in photos, or even in numbers. At Baseball Prospectus, we understand that statistics don't replace observation or any of baseball's stories, but complement everything else that makes the game so much fun.

What stats help us with is with patterns and precision, variance and value. This book can help you learn things you may not see from watching a game or hundred, whether it's the path of a career over time or the breadth of the entire MLB. We'd also never ask you to choose between our numbers and the experience of viewing a game from the cheap seats or the comfort of your home; our publication combines running the numbers with observations and wisdom from some of the brightest minds we can find. But if you *do* want to learn more about the numbers beyond what's on the backs of player jerseys, let us help explain.

Offense

At the end of this past year, we've revised our methodology for determining batting value. Long-time readers of Baseball Prospectus will notice that we've retired True Average in favor of a new metric: Deserved Runs Created Plus (DRC+). Developed by Jonathan Judge and our stats team, this statistic measures everything a player does at the plate–reaching base, hitting for power, making outs, and moving runners over–and puts it on a scale where 100 equals league-average performance. A DRC+ of 150 is terrific, a DRC+ of 100 is average, and a DRC+ of 75 means you better be an excellent defender.

DRC+ also does a better job than any of our previous metrics in taking contextual factors into account. The model adjusts for how the park affects performance, but also for things like the talent of the opposing pitcher, value of different types of batted-ball events, league, temperature, and other factors. It's able to describe a player's expected offensive contribution than any other statistic we've found over the years, and also does a better job of predicting future performance as well.

The other aspect of run-scoring is baserunning, which we quantify using Baserunning Runs. BRR not only records the value of stolen bases (or getting caught in the act), but also accounts for a runner's ability to go first to third on a single or advance on a fly ball.

Defense

Where offensive value is *relatively* easy to identify and understand, defensive value is ... not. Over the past dozen years, the sabermetric community has focused mostly on stats based on zone data: a real-live human person records the type of batted ball and estimated landing location, and models are created that give expected outs. From there, you can compare fielders' actual outs to those expected ones. Simple, right?

Unfortunately, zone data has two major issues. First, zone data is recorded by commercial data providers who keep the raw data private unless you pay for it. (All the statistics we build in this book and on our website use public data as inputs.) That hurts our ability to test assumptions or duplicate results. Second, over the years it has become apparent that there's quite a bit of "noise" in zone-based fielding analysis. Sometimes the conclusions drawn from zone data don't hold up to scrutiny, and sometimes the different data provided by different providers don't look anything alike, giving wildly different results. Sometimes the hard-working professional stringers or scorers might unknowingly inflict unconscious bias into the mix: for example good fielders will often be credited with more expected outs despite the data, and ballparks with high press boxes tend to score more line drives than ones with a lower press box.

Enter our Fielding Runs Above Average (FRAA). For most positions, FRAA is built from play-by-play data, which allows us to avoid the subjectivity found in many other fielding metrics. The idea is this: count how many fielding plays are made by a given player and compare that to expected plays for an average fielder at their position (based on pitcher ground-ball tendencies and batter handedness). Then we adjust for park and base-out situations.

When it comes to catchers, our methodology is a little different thanks to the laundry list of responsibilities they're tasked with beyond just, well, catching and throwing the ball. By now you've probably heard about "framing" or the art of making umpires more likely to call balls outside the strike zone for strikes. To put this into one tidy number, we incorporate pitch tracking data (for the years it exists) and adjust for important factors like pitcher, umpire, batter, and home-field advantage using a mixed-model approach. This grants us a number for how many strikes the catcher is personally adding to (or subtracting from) his pitchers' performance ... which we then convert to runs added or lost using linear weights.

Framing is one of the biggest parts of determining catcher value, but we also take into account blocking balls from going past, whether a scorer deems it a passed ball or a wild pitch. We use a similar approach–one that really benefits from the pitch tracking data that tells us what ends up in the dirt and what doesn't. We also include a catcher's ability to prevent stolen bases and how well they field balls in play, and *finally* we come up with our FRAA for catchers.

Pitching

Both pitching and fielding make up the half of baseball that isn't run scoring: run prevention. Separating pitching from fielding is a tough task, and most recent pitching analysis has branched off from Voros McCracken's famous (and controversial) statement, "There is little if any difference among major-league pitchers in their ability to prevent hits on balls hit in the field of play." The research of the analytic community has validated this to some extent, and there are a host of "defense-independent" pitching measures that have been developed to try and extricate the effect of the defense behind a hurler from the pitcher's work.

Our solution to this quandry is Deserved Run Average (DRA), our core pitching metric. DRA looks like earned run average (ERA), the tried-and-true pitching stat you've seen on every baseball broadcast or box score from the past century, but it's very different. To start, DRA takes an event-by-event look at what the pitchers does, and adjusts the value of that event based on different environmental factors like park, batter, catcher, umpire, base-out situation, run differential, inning, defense, home field advantage, pitcher role, and temperature. That mixed model gives us a pitcher's expected contribution, similar to what we do for our DRC+ model for hitters and FRAA model for catchers. (Oh, and we also consider the pitcher's effect on basestealing and on balls getting past the catcher.)

It's important to note that DRA is set to the scale of runs allowed per nine innings (RA9) instead of ERA, which makes DRA's scale slightly higher than ERA's. The reason for this is because ERA tends to overrate three types of pitchers:

1. Pitchers who play in parks where scorers hand out more errors. Official scorers differ significantly in the frequency at which they assign errors to fielders.
2. Ground-ball pitchers, because a substantial proportion of errors occur on grounders.
3. Pitchers who aren't very good. Better pitchers often allow fewer unearned runs than bad pitchers, because good pitchers tend to find ways to get out of jams.

Since the last time you picked up an edition of this book, we've also made a few minor changes to DRA to make it better. Recent research into "tunneling"–the act of throwing consecutive pitches that appear similar from a batter's point of view until after the swing decision point–data has given us a new contextual factor to account for in DRA: plate distance. This refers to the distance between successive pitches as they approach the plate, and while it has a smaller effect than factors like velocity or whiff rate, it still can help explain pitcher strikeout rate in our model.

New Pitching Metrics for 2019

We're including a few "new" pitching metrics for 2019's suite of Baseball Prospectus publications, but you may be familiar with them if you've spent time scouring the internet for stats.

Fastball Percentage

Our fastball percentage (FB%) statistic measures how frequently a pitcher throws a pitch classified as a "fastball," measured as a percentage of overall pitches thrown. We qualify three types of fastballs:

1. The traditional four-seam fastball;
2. The two-seam fastball or sinker;
3. "Hard cutters," which are pitches that have the movement profile of a cut fastball and are used as the pitcher's primary offering or in place of a more traditional fastball.

For example, a pitcher with a FB% of 67 throws any combination of these three pitches about two-thirds of the time.

Whiff Rate

Everybody loves a swing and a miss, and whiff rate (WHF) measures how frequently pitchers induce a swinging strike. To calculate WHF, we add up all the pitches thrown that ended with a swinging strike, then divide that number by a pitcher's total pitches thrown. Most often, high whiff rates correlate with high strikeout rates (and overall effective pitcher performance).

Called Strike Probability

Called Strike Probability (CSP) is a number that represents the likelihood that all of a pitcher's pitches will be called a strike while controlling for location, pitcher and batter handedness, umpire and count. Here's how it works: on each pitch, our model determines how many times (out of 100) that a similar pitch was called for a strike given those factors mentioned above, and when normalized for each batter's strike zone. Then we average the CSP for all pitches thrown by a pitcher in a season, and that gives us the yearly CSP percentage you see in the stats boxes.

As you might imagine, pitchers with a higher CSP are more likely to work in the zone, where pitchers with a lower CSP are likely locating their pitches outside the normal strike zone, for better or for worse.

Projections

Many of you aren't turning to this book just for a look at what a player has done, but for a look at what a player is going to do: the PECOTA projections. PECOTA, initially developed by Nate Silver (who has moved on to greater fame as a political analyst), consists of three parts:

1. Major-league equivalencies, which use minor-league statistics to project how a player will perform in the major leagues;
2. Baseline forecasts, which use weighted averages and regression to the mean to estimate a player's current true talent level; and
3. Aging curves, which uses the career paths of comparable players to estimate how a player's statistics are likely to change over time.

With all those important things covered, let's take a look at what's in the book this year.

Team Prospectus

You bought this book to learn more about your favorite (or maybe least-favorite, who are we to judge?) team, so let's talk about them. After a thoughtful preview of the 2019 season, you'll be presented with our Team Prospectus. This outlines many of the key statistics for each team's 2018 season, as well as a very inviting stadium diagram.

First you'll find the Performance Graphs page. The first is the 2018 Hit List Ranking. This shows our Hit List Rank for the team on each day of the 2018 season and is intended to give you a picture of the ups and downs of the team's season, including their highest and lowest ranks of the year. Hit List Rank measures overall team performance and drives the Hit List Power Rankings at the baseballprospectus.com website.

The second graph is Committed Payroll and helps you see how the team's payroll has compared to the MLB and divisional average payrolls over time. Payroll figures are currents as of January 1, 2019; with so many free agents still unsigned as of this writing, the final 2018 figure will likely be significantly different for many teams. (In the meantime, you can always find the most current data at Baseball Prospectus' Cot's Baseball Contracts page.)

Philadelphia Phillies 2019

The third graph is Farm System Ranking and displays how the Baseball Prospectus prospect team has ranked the organization's farm system since 2007. It also indicates the highest and lowest ranks that the farm system achieved over that time.

We start the Team Performance page with the squad's unadjusted and third-order 2018 win-loss records, presented in divisional context. We then list the three highest performing hitters and pitchers by WARP for 2018. Beneath that are a host of other team statistics. **Pythag** presents an adjusted 2018 winning percentage, calculated by taking runs scored per game (**RS/G**) and runs allowed per game (**RA/G**) for the team, and running them through a version of Bill James' Pythagorean formula that was refined and improved by David Smyth and Brandon Heipp. (The formula is called "Pythagenpat," which is equally fun to type and to say.)

Next up is **DRC+**, described earlier, to indicate the overall hitting ability of the team either above or below league-average. Run prevention on the pitching side is covered by **DRA** (also mentioned earlier) and another metric: Fielding Independent Pitching (**FIP**), which calculates another ERA-like statistic based on strikeouts, walks, and home runs recorded. Defensive Efficiency Rating (**DER**) tells us the percentage of balls in play turned into outs for the team, and is a quick fielding shorthand that rounds out run prevention.

After that, we have several measures related to roster composition, as opposed to on-field performance. **B-Age** and **P-Age** tell us the average age of a team's batters and pitchers, respectively. **Salary** is the combined team payroll for all on-field players, and Doug Pappas' Marginal Dollars per Marginal Win (**M$/MW**) tells us how much money a team spent to earn production above replacement level.

Ending this batch of statistics is the number of disabled list days a team had over the season (**DL Days**) and the amount of salary paid to players on the disabled list (**$ on DL**); this final number is expressed as a percentage of total payroll.

Next to each of these stats, we've listed each team's MLB rank in that category from 1st to 30th. In this, 1st always indicates a positive outcome and 30th a negative outcome, except in the case of salary–1st is highest.

The Team Projections page is intended to convey the team's operational capacity entering the 2019 season. We start with the team's PECOTA projected record for 2019, again in divisional context. The **+/-** column indicates how many more or less wins the team is projected to get than they got in 2018. We then list the three highest projected hitters and pitchers by WARP for 2018. A brief farm system summary follows, with the team's top prospect and number of BP Top 101 Prospects. Finally, we list the key new players and departed players, along with their 2019 projected WARP.

www.baseballprospectus.com

Alex Bregman 3B

Born: 03/30/94 Age: 25 Bats: R Throws: R
Height: 6'0" Weight: 180 Origin: Round 1, 2015 Draft (#2 overall)

YEAR	TEAM	LVL	AGE	PA	R	2B	3B	HR	RBI	BB	K	SB	CS	AVG/OBP/SLG
2016	CCH	AA	22	285	54	16	2	14	46	42	26	5	3	.297/.415/.559
2016	FRE	AAA	22	83	17	6	0	6	15	5	12	2	1	.333/.373/.641
2016	HOU	MLB	22	217	31	13	3	8	34	15	52	2	0	.264/.313/.478
2017	HOU	MLB	23	626	88	39	5	19	71	55	97	17	5	.284/.352/.475
2018	HOU	MLB	24	705	105	51	1	31	103	96	85	10	4	.286/.394/.532
2019	HOU	MLB	25	675	96	38	3	23	78	73	107	12	4	.272/.359/.463

Breakout: 6% Improve: 52% Collapse: 5% Attrition: 2% MLB: 100%
Comparables: Anthony Rendon, David Wright, Pablo Sandoval

YEAR	TEAM	LVL	AGE	PA	DRC+	VORP	BABIP	BRR	FRAA	WARP
2016	CCH	AA	22	285	172	38.9	.286	1.6	SS(51): -3.4, 3B(11): 1.4	2.7
2016	FRE	AAA	22	83	161	10.0	.333	-1.2	SS(14): 2.1, LF(3): -0.1	0.8
2016	HOU	MLB	22	217	107	9.6	.317	0.5	3B(40): 0.9, SS(6): -0.1	1.1
2017	HOU	MLB	23	626	114	34.7	.311	-1.5	3B(132): 8.7, SS(30): -2.9	3.9
2018	HOU	MLB	24	705	150	72.6	.289	-1.6	3B(136): 5.4, SS(28): -0.4	7.4
2019	HOU	MLB	25	675	125	37.3	.295	0.0	3B 7, SS 0	4.6

After the projections page, we share a few items about the team's home ballpark. There's the aforementioned diagram of the park's dimensions (including distances to the outfield wall), a few important biographical facts about the stadium, a graphic showing the height of the wall from the left-field pole to the right-field pole, and a table showing three-year park factors for the stadium. The park factors are displayed as indexes where 100 is average, 110 means that the park inflates the statistic in question by 10 percent, and 90 means that the park deflates the statistic in question by 10 percent.

Following the ballpark page, we have a **Personnel** section that lists many of the important decision-makers and upper-level field and operations staff members for the franchise, as well as any former Baseball Prospectus staff members who are currently part of the organization.

Position Players

After all that information and a thoughtful bylined essay covering each team, we present our player comments. Each player is listed with the major-league team who employed him as of early January 2019. If a player changed teams after that point via free agency, trade, or any other method, you'll be able to find them in the book for their previous squad.

First, we cover biographical information (age is as of June 30, 2019) before moving onto the stats themselves. Our statistic columns include standard identifying information like **YEAR**, **TEAM**, **LVL** (level of affiliated play) and **AGE**

Statistical Introduction - xiii

before getting into the numbers. Next, we provide raw, unstranslated numbers like you might find on the back of your dad's baseball cards: **PA** (plate appearances), **R** (runs), **2B** (doubles), **3B** (triples), **HR** (home runs), **RBI** (runs batted in), **BB** (walks), **K** (strikeouts), **SB** (stolen bases) and **CS** (caught stealing). Then we have unadjusted "slash" statistics: **AVG** (batting average), **OBP** (on-base percentage) and **SLG** (slugging percentage).

Just below the stats box is **PECOTA** data, which is discussed further in a following section. After that, it's on to a pithy and always-informative comment written by a member of the Baseball Prospectus staff, before we cover more stats.

The second text box repeats YEAR, TEAM, LVL, AGE, and PA, then moves on to **DRC+** (Deserved Runs Created Plus), which we described earlier as total offensive expected contribution compared to the league average. Next, one of our oldest active metrics, **VORP** (Value Over Replacement Player), considers offensive production, position and plate appearances. In essence, it is the number of runs contributed beyond what a replacement-level player at the same position would contribute if given the same percentage of team plate appearances. VORP does not consider the quality of a player's defense.

BABIP (batting average on balls in play) tells us how often a ball in play fell for a hit, and can help us identify whether a batter may have been lucky or not ... but note that high BABIPs also tend to follow the great hitters of our time, as well as speedy singles hitters who put the ball on the ground.

The next item is **BRR** (Baserunning Runs), which covers all of a player's baserunning accomplishments which includes (but isn't limited to) swiped bags and failed attempts. Next is **FRAA** (Fielding Runs Above Average), which also includes the number of games previously played at each position noted in parentheses. Multi-position players have only their two most frequent positions listed here, but their total FRAA number reflects all positions played.

Our last column here is **WARP** (Wins Above Replacement Player). WARP estimates the total value of a player, which means for hitters it takes into account hitting runs above average (calculated using the DRC+ model), BRR and FRAA. Then, it makes an adjustment for positions played and gives the player a credit for plate appearances based upon the difference between "replacement level"¬–which is derived from the quality of players added to a team's roster after the start of the season¬–and the league average.

Catchers

Catchers are a special breed, and thus they have earned their own separate box which displays some of the defensive metrics that we've built just for them. As an example, let's check out J.T. Realmuto.

www.baseballprospectus.com

YEAR	TEAM	P. COUNT	FRM RUNS	BLK RUNS	THRW RUNS	TOT RUNS
2016	MIA	18935	-8.5	1.8	2.1	-5.6
2017	MIA	18959	5.3	1.7	1.0	9.1
2018	MIA	16399	-0.4	0.9	0.1	0.4
2019	PHI	18448	-1.4	1.5	0.7	0.8

The **YEAR** and **TEAM** columns match what you'd find in the other stat box. **P. COUNT** indicates the number of pitches thrown while the catcher was behind the plate, including swinging strikes, fouls, and balls in play. **FRM RUNS** is the total run value the catcher provided (or cost) his team by influencing the umpire to call strikes where other catchers did not. **BLK RUNS** expresses the total run value above or below average for the catcher's ability to prevent wild pitches and passed balls. **THRW RUNS** is calculated using a similar model as the previous two statistics, and it measures a catcher's ability to throw out basestealers but also to dissuade them from testing his arm in the first place. It takes into account factors like the pitcher (including his delivery and pickoff move) and baserunner (who could be as fast as Billy Hamilton or as slow as Yonder Alonso). **TOT RUNS** is the sum of all of the previous three statistics.

Pitchers

Let's give our pitchers a turn, using 2018 NL Cy Young winner Jacob deGrom as our example. Take a look at his first stat block: the first line and the **YEAR**, **TEAM**, **LVL** and **AGE** columns are the same as in the position player example earlier.

Here too, we have a series of columns that display raw, unadjusted statistics compiled by the pitcher over the course of a season: **W** (wins), **L** (losses), **SV** (saves), **G** (games pitched), **GS** (games started), **IP** (innings pitched), **H** (hits allowed) and **HR** (home runs allowed). Next we have two statistics that are rates: **BB/9** (walks per nine innings) and **K/9** (strikeouts per nine innings), before returning to the unadjusted **K** (strikeouts).

Next up is **GB%** (ground ball percentage), which is the percentage of all batted balls that were hit in the ground, including both outs and hits. Remember, this is based on observational data and subject to human error, so please approach this with a healthy dose of skepticism.

BABIP (batting average on balls in play) is calculated using the same methodology as it is for position players, but it often tells us more about a pitcher than it does a hitter. With pitchers, a high BABIP is often due to poor defense or bad luck, and can often be an indicator of potential rebound, and a low BABIP may be cause to expect performance regression. (A typical league-average BABIP is close to .290-.300.)

After a witty 150ish words on the player like only Baseball Prospectus's staff can provide, it's on to that second stat block, which repeats the YEAR, TEAM, LVL, and AGE columns. The metrics **WHIP** (walks plus hits per inning pitched) and **ERA**

Statistical Introduction - xv

Philadelphia Phillies 2019

(earned run average) are old standbys: WHIP measures walks and hits allowed on a per-inning basis, while ERA measures earned runs on a nine-inning basis. Neither of these stats are translated or adjusted.

DRA (Deserved Run Average) was described at length earlier, and measures how many runs the pitcher "deserved" to allow per nine innings. Please note that since we lack all the data points that would make for a "real" DRA for minor-league events, the DRA displayed for minor league partial-seasons is based off of different data. (That data is a modified version of our cFIP metric, which you can find more information about on our website.)

Jacob deGrom   RHP
Born: 06/19/88   Age: 31   Bats: L   Throws: R
Height: 6'4"   Weight: 180   Origin: Round 9, 2010 Draft (#272 overall)

YEAR	TEAM	LVL	AGE	W	L	SV	G	GS	IP	H	HR	BB/9	K/9	K	GB%	BABIP
2016	NYN	MLB	28	7	8	0	24	24	148	142	15	2.2	8.7	143	47%	.312
2017	NYN	MLB	29	15	10	0	31	31	201^1	180	28	2.6	10.7	239	48%	.305
2018	NYN	MLB	30	10	9	0	32	32	217	152	10	1.9	11.2	269	48%	.281
2019	NYN	MLB	31	13	9	0	31	31	186	145	18	2.3	10.7	221	46%	.286

Breakout: 8%   Improve: 29%   Collapse: 28%   Attrition: 6%   MLB: 85%
Comparables: Erik Bedard, A.J. Burnett, CC Sabathia

YEAR	TEAM	LVL	AGE	WHIP	ERA	DRA	WARP	MPH	FB%	WHF	CSP
2016	NYN	MLB	28	1.20	3.04	3.30	3.5	96.3	59.6	12.1	47.2
2017	NYN	MLB	29	1.19	3.53	3.02	5.7	97.2	55.5	14.5	49.5
2018	NYN	MLB	30	0.91	1.70	2.09	8.0	98.2	52.1	16.3	48.4
2019	NYN	MLB	31	1.02	2.91	3.23	3.9	96.6	54.5	14.8	48.2

Just like with hitters, **WARP** (Wins Above Replacement Player) is a total value metric that puts pitchers of all stripes on the same scale as position players. We use DRA as the primary input for our calculation of WARP. You might notice that relief pitchers (due to their limited innings) may have a lower WARP than you were expecting or than you might see in other WARP-like metrics. WARP does not take leverage into account, just the actions a pitcher performs and the expected value of those actions ... which ends up judging high-leverage relief pitchers differently than you might imagine given their prestige and market value.

MPH gives you the pitcher's 95th percentile velocity for the noted season, in order to give you an idea of what the *peak* fastball velocity a pitcher possesses. Since this comes from our pitch tracking data, it is not publicly available for minor-league pitchers.

Finally, we display the three new pitching metrics we described earlier. **FB%** (fastball percentage) gives you the percentage of fastballs thrown out of all pitches. **WhiffRt** (whiff rate) tells you the percentage of swinging strikes induced out of all pitches. **CS Prob** (called strike probability) expresses the likelihood of all pitches thrown to result in a called strike, after controlling for factors like handedness, umpire, pitch type, count, and location.

PECOTA

All players have PECOTA projections for 2019, as well as a set of other numbers that describe the performance of comparable players according to PECOTA. All projections for 2019 are for the player at the date we went to press in early January and are projected into the league and park context as indicated by the team abbreviation. All PECOTA projected statistics represent a player's projected major-league performance.

The numbers beneath the player's stats–Breakout, Improve, Collapse, Attrition–are part and parcel of the PECOTA projections. They estimate the likelihood of changes in performance relative to the player's previously-established level of production, based on the performance of comparable players:

Breakout Rate is the percent change that a player's production will improve by at least 20 percent relative to the weighted average of his performance over his most recent seasons.

Improve Rate is the percent chance that a player's production will improve at all relative to his baseline performance. A player who is expected to perform just the same as he has in the recent past will have an Improve Rate of 50 percent.

Collapse Rate is the percent chance that a position player's production will decline by at least 25 percent relative to his baseline performance.

Attrition Rate operates on playing time rather than performance. Specifically, it measures the likelihood that a player's playing time will decrease by at least 50 percent relative to his established level.

Breakout Rate and Collapse Rate can sometimes be counterintuitive for players who have already experienced a radical change in performance level. It's also worth noting that the projected decline in a player's rate performances might not be indicative of an expected decline in underlying ability or skill, but could just be an anticipated correction following a breakout season.

MLB% is the percentage of similar players who played in the major leagues in their relevant season.

The final pieces of information are the player's three highest-scoring comparable players as determined by PECOTA. All comparables represent a snapshot of how the listed player was performing at the same age as the current player, so if a 23-year-old pitcher is compared to Bartolo Colon, he's actually being compared to a 23-year-old Colon, not the version that pitched for the Rangers in 2018, nor to Colon's career as a whole.

Statistical Introduction - xvii

A few points about pitcher projections. First, we aren't yet projecting peak velocity, so that column will be blank in the PECOTA lines. Second, projecting DRA is trickier than evaluating past performance, because it is unclear how deserving each pitcher will be of his anticipated outcomes. However, we know that another DRA-related statistic–contextual FIP or cFIP–estimates future run scoring very well. So for PECOTA, the projected DRA figures you see are based on the past cFIPs generated by the pitcher and comparable players over time, along with the other factors described above.

Lineouts

In each chapter's Lineouts section, you'll find abbreviated text comments, as well as most of same information you'd find in our full player comments. We limit the stats boxes in this section to only including the 2018 information for each player.

Exclusive Player Visualizations

In our constant battle to provide you with new and interesting baseball content you can't find anywhere else, we've added a trio of data visualizations to each hitter's entry in these books and a pair of visualizations for each pitcher.

For hitters, you'll find three new infographics. The first is each player's **Batted Ball Distribution**, which displays the five major sections of the field: LF (left), LCF (left center), CF (center), RCF (right center), and RF (right). The percentage indicated tells us what percentage of batted balls from that hitter fell within that part of the field during the 2018 season. We've also included the hitter's slugging percentage on balls in play (also called **SLGCON**) for that part of the field.

You'll also see two heatmaps: **Strike Zone vs LHP** and **Strike Zone vs RHP**. These heat maps represent a view of the strike zone from behind the catcher. Areas where there is a darker coloration represent the places where a higher percentage of pitches resulted in hits. In other words, the heatmap represents a hitter's "sweet spots" for getting hits against either left-handed or right-handed pitchers, depending on the image.

Pitchers get two images that help explain what their pitches look like from a hitter's perspective: **Pitch Shape vs LHH** and **Pitch Shape vs RHH**. These images show you the shape and the "tunneling" effect of each pitcher's offerings from the batter's perspective. For each type of pitch that a pitcher throws (represented by an indicator shape), there's a set of dots indicating the flight path, where each dot represents a 0.01-second interval. This maps the average trajectory and speed of an offering, ending where the ball crosses the plate. The solid black box represents the regular strike zone, while the gray contour lines indicate the range of locations that a pitcher typically works in.

Below the image, we provide a bit more detailed information about each pitcher's average offering in the **Pitch Types** box. Here, we also list each of the pitcher's major offerings under the **Type** column.

- **Fastballs** (which usually refers to the four-seam variation)
- **Sinkers** and/or two-seam fastballs
- **Cutters** (which could include "hard" cutters like cut fastballs and "soft" cutters that resemble hard sliders)
- **Changeups** (not including most splitters)
- **Splitters** (split-fingered pitches, forkballs, and some split-changes)
- **Sliders** and/or slurves
- **Curveballs** (including spike-curveballs and knuckle-curveballs, as well as some slurvy curves)
- **Slow curveballs** and/or eephus pitches
- **Knuckleballs**
- **Screwballs**

The **Freq** column indicates the percentage of overall pitches that fall into each of those type categories; if a pitcher has a 16.55% score for changeups, then that's the percent of all pitches that he throws as changeups. **Velo** is exactly what you think it is: the average miles per hour for each pitch type. **H Mov** is the number of inches of horizontal movement on the average pitch of that type, while **V Mov** is the number of inches of vertical movement on the average pitch of that type. (At Baseball Prospectus, we measure this over the long flight of the ball and include gravity into the V Mov number in order to give you the most realistic representation of what the pitch *actually* does.)

If you're wondering about the second number in brackets, that's the index for that velocity or movement compared to the league average. Like DRC+, a score of 100 means that the speed or movement is about the same as league average, while a higher score means that there's higher velocity or movement than the league average. Numbers below 100 indicate less velocity or movement than the league average.

Part 1: Team Analysis

Table for Two: Previewing the 2019 Philadelphia Phillies

Paul Boyé and Justin Klugh

JUSTIN KLUGH: Paul, we've both been watching and writing about the Phillies for a long time. We've sat through plenty of offseasons in which the Phillies have been involved in exactly nothing. Throughout this one, they've been at the center of just about every rumor, and yet you could stuff a couch with the hair we've pulled out of our heads in frustration. My question for you is, in a few years, do you think anyone will remember this winter as particularly unbearable, or will it slip into the same collective amnesia of every offseason we've ever experienced?

PAUL BOYE: Oh, this one's going into the memory banks either way. Think about this: Bryce Harper, the face of a division rival for seven years and a National League MVP at the age when he otherwise might have been graduating from college, joins the Phillies. An x-year deal for y dollars. He's either good, or he's bad, but either way, we'll always remember that we landed a superstar… the only thing in question would be the amount of derision in our voices. And if the Phillies miss? Do we expect Philly fans to up and forget someone who would so callously, egregiously, villainously toss them aside in such a way after that kind of wait? Hoo boy.

JUSTIN: I almost think people would *prefer* to be spurned by Harper. We haven't had a good old fashioned spurning in Philadelphia baseball for some time, and I've got a drawer full of expired batteries that I, according to a city charter, can *only* dispose of by hurling at a perceived enemy or face significant jail time.

That being said, I'm excited. There's a lot of good players on this team, even without the addition of Harper. I look forward to seeing what Jean Segura can do with runners in scoring position, and how J.T. Realmuto handles the dimensions of his new home park–he's slashed .282/.312/.476 with 4 HR there over his career, and it's well known how well he hit outside Marlins Park last year (.283/.350/.520, 13 HR in 254 AB).

But I also feel like this could be the year we see some sustained success out of Rhys Hoskins, because, frankly… why couldn't it be? He's yet to play a full season in which he was not out of position or broken-jawed or suddenly hitting .215 for a significant portion. On the other hand, he's the fastest Phillies player in history to reach 30 home runs and 100 walks, and he went on that torrid tater rampage during his rookie campaign that made him a Delaware Valley household name. It's obvious Hoskins is something special, but it feels like each time we're about to see him really take off, something gets in the way.

PAUL: We still don't know exactly what kind of hitter Hoskins is in terms of triple slash—his 2018 was a composite of an extreme hot-and-cold streaks, like you said—but we do know at this point that he's the anchor. He's the face of the team, with a friendly personality to match. He's even, apparently, an awesome recruiter, at least if you ask Realmuto about their trip to play in the Japan Series last fall. He doesn't *need* be anything more than a "pretty good" player if he's supplemented by the right supporting cast, and although adding Harper and/or Manny Machado certainly wouldn't hurt the cause, they've definitely done a good job fitting some pieces together already.

My big concern is—as it has been for, oh, about seven years now—is the pitching. The bullpen looks good and incredibly deep. But beyond (the newly extended) Aaron Nola, does this team have the rotation arms to hang with the Nationals and Mets?

JUSTIN: No, right? This team's efforts to fortify its starting pitching staff culminated in signing Jake Arrieta last February, and that paid off for about two non-consecutive months of elite pitching before he stopped missing bats and continued having a poor defense behind him, which led to him becoming one of this team's suspected off-the-record malcontents. And that one time, on the record.

I feel like we've been asking questions about the back-of-the-rotation gang for three years now, waiting for Vince Velasquez or Zach Eflin or Nick Pivetta to emerge and become a reliable presence, but once again I'm not sure who it will be.

Eflin's season, which started in May, had a definitive midpoint in which he got his ERA under 3.00 before that walk total started ballooning again. Velasquez is such a weapon, but once again we saw him burn through 50 or 60 pitches in two or three innings too many times. Jerad Eickhoff has lingering health issues. Enyel De Los Santos is still pretty raw. Ranger Suarez spread 15 innings over four big league games last year. There's the seemingly default choice of Dallas Keuchel on the free agent market, but word is, people are buying stock in Nick Pivetta in 2019.

PAUL: Like me! I'm doing that! From his 2018 K%-BB% (19.7) on down through DRA (3.40), Nick Pivetta is the statistical breakout darling of 2019. If he fails to break out, the entire statistical movement in baseball will have been a failure.

In reality, though, you're right. This is not a team with a starting rotation that will make you worry about how your offense will hang in for six innings on most nights. What this team *does* have, though, is a stellar bullpen. Seranthony

Dominguez has the stuff to be an absolutely insane reliever; David Robertson has been steady-as-she-goes for a decade; hell, one of the game's more promising young RPs, Victor Arano, might get squeezed out to start the year because he's one of the few guys left with options. That's what it's come to! They may not feature a Scherzer/Strasburg one-two punch, but the Phillies have a whole bunch of guys who throw the baseball pretty well all the same. And that might be what keeps them in the hunt this summer.

JUSTIN: There's something so warm and comforting about a promising bullpen stacked with arms. That one-two punch exists, just at the end of the game, not the front, like you said, with Dominguez and Robertson. Dominguez appeared in 53 games last year and allowed earned runs in only ten of them; Robertson has been showing up in 60-70 games a season since 2010, typically generating 1-2 WAR all on his own. But you don't want to have to tap into your best weapons too early—we saw what happened last year when Kapler tried to turn relievers like Dominguez into two-inning pitchers just because he wanted them to be.

Which kind of brings me to my next point: What do we have in sophomore year Gabe Kapler? This is a guy who claimed how open to change he was, but also appeared at times to be a chronic over-manager in 2018. His analytic reputation has split off of him and become an entity of its own at this point. I think he knows how to call relievers into the game now, but I guess the question is, does he have a team that's better equipped to fit the way he wants to manage? Is this "Gabe Kapler's team?"

PAUL: I never know how to judge managers. There's so much that goes into game prep beyond what we can see that I eventually just admitted to myself that I'd be bad at truly understanding what it takes to be a good Major League manager.

What we *do* hear and see is that Kapler has the public support of Rhys Hoskins, and that's a huge chip in his stack. Hoskins is sort of this unifying force in Philadelphia, a uniter of a fanbase regardless of old- or new-school mindset. Having him back Kapler is a necessary stabilizer while this team tries to figure out if he's championship caliber; or, at least, stays out of the way enough to let the players be championship caliber. At the end of the day, a manager is only as good as the players he can deploy.

His players are better this year, so the team should be better. Is it wrong to think that simply?

JUSTIN: No, and it's tough not to. At many points this winter, we've had to separate ourselves from any Phillies/Harper/Machado talk, because it has gone on for so long and has become so inane. Doing so forces you to look at the team *without* one of the megastars we've waited for, and to be honest, it's not a bad looking group.

I don't want to echo Andy MacPhail from his press conference, because this front office does *not* deserve a pat on the back for having Harper within reach, as well as the funds to pay him, as well a position at which to play him, as well as an offense in desperate need of him, and *not* acquiring him, just because they traded for J.T. Realmuto and put a Shake Shack by the third base gate. It *is* fair to say that this team is a lot better than last year at this point, because it's inarguably true.

But remember how Matt Klentak came out at the end of last season–and MacPhail just cited this again too–and said that look, this team improved by 16 wins? That's a fun way of saying they went from 66 to 80 wins, but even so, neither of those teams made the playoffs–that 2017 team only scored 690 runs, and their 2018 counterparts scored even fewer (677). This team has taken great strides, but they've had to keep defending themselves against criticism that it's not enough, because people don't want a team that's a little further out of a hole. They want a team that's not in one.

Somewhere around "stupid money," expectations went into the stratosphere, and I don't know when they'll come back down. By all means, the Phillies have improved their team, and I think it's good enough as is to compete for an accidental wild card spot. But even without Harper, they still need starting pitching, they still need bench depth, they still need something real for Scott Kingery to do. The Phillies were so bad for most of a decade that a good team can be made to look great by comparison. And that's, to use a technical term, weak sauce, when they could have been objectively the best (on paper).

I've inadvertently given my prediction for this squad as it stands now: 86-76, ass-backwards wild card spot contender. Where do you have them?

PAUL: I am always SO BAD at predictions. You're better off reincarnating that octopus that predicted World Cup matches in 2010 to take a stab at this than you are asking me.

But let's do this anyway. I actually like where the pitching is at—even if you're not as high on, say, Pivetta as I am, it's nice to have a boatload of relievers to mitigate the pain of short starts here and there—and think the offense is a mile ahead of 2018 even before a more significant add. They'll hit depth problems if an infielder or catcher (gulp) goes down for an extended period. Seriously; having Realmuto here is awesome, but the drop from him and his 122 DRC+ to whatever it is we might be expecting from Andrew Knapp or Drew Butera is… precipitous. So health is even more crucial for this team than usual.

Now, the rest of the division made some moves, too. It was an active offseason for everyone, even if volume doesn't always equate with dramatic improvement. Each of the teams still has questions, and I'm of the mind that there won't be a runaway division winner this year.

I think the Phillies are a toss-up second-or-third-place team right now. Crossing .500 is a very reasonable ask, but 90 wins might be out of reach. We'll see where they are in July and who might be available for trade, but as we type here today, I think this team just misses the playoffs. 84-78.

I hope your crystal ball is less smudgy than mine.

Performance Graphs

2018 Hit List Ranking

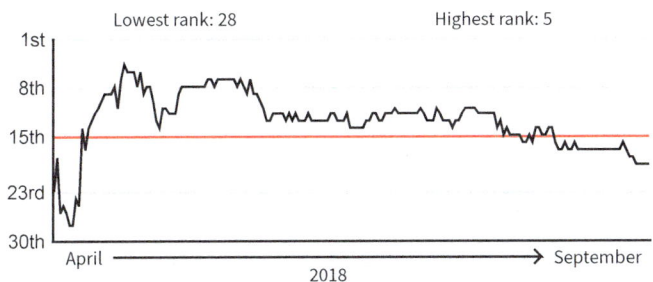

Committed Payroll (in millions)

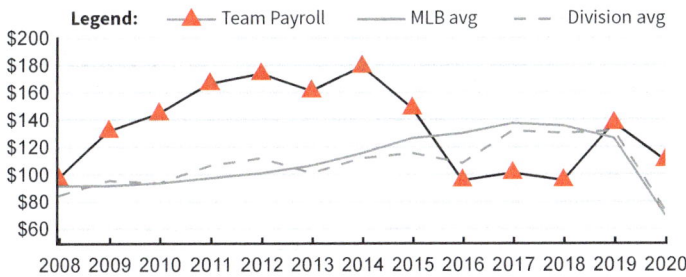

Farm System Ranking

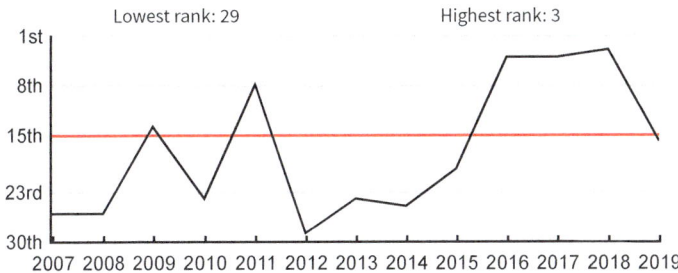

2018 Team Performance

ACTUAL STANDINGS

Team	W	L	Pct
ATL	90	72	.555
WAS	82	80	.506
PHI	**80**	**82**	**.493**
NYN	77	85	.475
MIA	63	98	.391

THIRD-ORDER STANDINGS

Team	W	L	Pct
ATL	94	68	.580
WAS	91	71	.561
NYN	79	83	.487
PHI	**79**	**83**	**.487**
MIA	63	98	.391

TOP HITTERS

Player	WARP
Rhys Hoskins	3.9
Cesar Hernandez	2.9
Jorge Alfaro	2.5

TOP PITCHERS

Player	WARP
Aaron Nola	6.6
Nick Pivetta	3.6
Jake Arrieta	2.4

VITAL STATISTICS

Statistic Name	Value	Rank
Pythagenpat	.466	20th
Runs Scored per Game	4.18	21st
Runs Allowed per Game	4.49	19th
Deserved Runs Created Plus	90	24th
Deserved Run Average	3.95	7th
Fielding Independent Pitching	3.79	4th
Defensive Efficiency Rating	.697	26th
Batter Age	26.7	2nd
Pitcher Age	26.6	3rd
Salary	$95.3M	24th
Marginal $ per Marginal Win	$2.6M	25th
Disabled List Days	$924.0M	9th
$ on DL	15%	13th

2019 Team Projections

PROJECTED STANDINGS

Team	W	L	Pct	+/-
WAS	89	73	.549	+7
NYN	87	75	.537	+10
ATL	85	77	.524	-5
PHI	**85**	**77**	**.524**	**+5**
MIA	68	94	.419	+5

TOP PROJECTED HITTERS

Player	WARP
Bryce Harper	3.6
J.T. Realmuto	3.4
Jean Segura	2.6

TOP PROJECTED PITCHERS

Player	WARP
Aaron Nola	4.0
Nick Pivetta	2.5
Jake Arrieta	1.6

FARM SYSTEM REPORT

Top Prospect	Number of Top 101 Prospects
Adonis Medina, #57	1

KEY DEDUCTIONS

Player	WARP
Carlos Santana	2.1
Wilson Ramos	1.8
Jorge Alfaro	1.1
Justin Bour	0.9
Asdrubal Cabrera	0.6
Luis Garcia	0.4

KEY ADDITIONS

Player	WARP
Bryce Harper	3.6
J.T. Realmuto	3.4
Jean Segura	2.6
Andrew McCutchen	2.5
David Robertson	0.8
Juan Nicasio	0.3

Team Personnel

President
Andy MacPhail

VP, General Manager
Matt Klentak

Assistant General Manager
Scott Proefrock

Assistant General Manager
Ned Rice

Manager
Gabe Kapler

BP Alumni
Lewie Pollis

Citizens Bank Park Stats

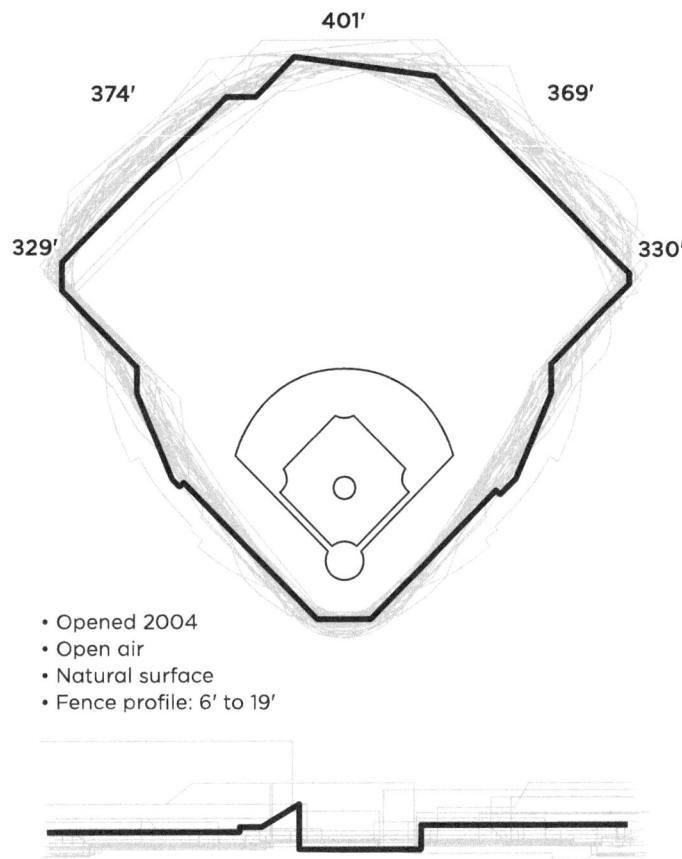

- Opened 2004
- Open air
- Natural surface
- Fence profile: 6' to 19'

Three-Year Park Factors

Runs	Runs/RH	Runs/LH	HR/RH	HR/LH
100	101	97	111	112

Phillies Team Analysis

There was once a young, inexperienced baseball man who came to Philadelphia to win it all.

He showed up and began unpacking some wacky ideas to gain a series of tiny advantages against his opponents that confused and enraged everyone watching. People thought him smug or strange; overcomplicating the game's purity by twisting knobs and pushing buttons. But it was in these narrow strategic margins that games were won or lost. One of his plans was to swap the placement of the Phillies' bullpen with their opponents' in order to increase their home field advantage. The idea was that it would allow his relievers a better angle to alert the third base coach if a batted ball was catchable or not by waving towels, gaining precious seconds for a runner.

As the legend goes, four years later, he proved his doubters wrong by managing one of the best Phillies teams of all time. As the legend continues, several weeks later, he proved his doubters right when that same team crumbled down the stretch and lost its playoff spot in the most baffling, demoralizing, and damaging collapse in the history of Philadelphia sports.

The point here, as Gene Mauch learned during that magical and then terrible 1964 season, is that in baseball, change is as inevitable as failure.

This past season, in 2018, another young, inexperienced baseball man arrived in Philadelphia with a monosyllabic name that starts with "G." Gabe Kapler brought some pretty wacky ideas with him, too. And once again, everything changed. Right before everything failed.

Over the winter, the Phillies had become ready to put a face on their franchise. They sent young slugger Rhys Hoskins across the street, with jackrabbit shortstop J.P. Crawford in tow, to ring the pregame bell at a Sixers game and wave to the crowd. "Here he is," the Phillies were saying, gesturing theatrically at Hoskins. "Philly's next baseball guy. Take down the faded Utley posters, gang; this one hits 'em long and walks a lot. Look at that smile. All right, have fun."

And then, the season began. Hoskins finished April hitting over .300, then plummeted from relevance. He then fouled a pitch off his jaw to close out May and came back with all of his power, crushing eight home runs with a .688 SLG in June. In July he went warm, in August he went cold, and in September he, like the rest of his teammates, was about as effective a hitter as Gene Mauch, who'd been dead for 13 years.

Philadelphia Phillies 2019

It wasn't just Hoskins. There was no impassioned speech or closed-door meeting that could rally this team by the season's final six weeks. The powerless offense waved feebly at pitches; the penetrable defense tumbled out of the way of ground balls; the roster lauded for its youthful outlook was now dotted with more veterans every night as extra parts like Asdrubal Cabrera, Jose Bautista, Wilson Ramos, and Justin Bour were added mid-season. Scott Kingery was tossed into a 24-4 August loss to the Mets for a garbage time pitching appearance and lobbed the ball so pathetically the stadium radar gun couldn't even pick it up. Focus wilted with each passing loss; just before the Phillies' penultimate game, Odubel Herrera and Dylan Cozens realized a moment before first pitch that they were in the wrong positions and had to switch spots.

The long baseball season chewed up this team, and exposed more of their weaknesses than there may have surfaced during a year in which they weren't simultaneously trying out new players, a new manager, and a new organizational mindset, all while John Middleton casually let it slip from the owner's box how much money he was going to spend in the most intimidating free agency class in franchise history.

Blame, in Philadelphia, flows hotter than the cheese steak grease. It splattered all over the Phillies, on the maddeningly inconsistent Odubel Herrera, on the maddeningly consistent Carlos Santana, on the consistently maddening Scott Kingery, on the bullpen, on the starters, on the front office, on math, on coconut oil—but the most hoarsely shouted name belonged to Gabe Kapler, the 43-year-old first-time manager with a penchant for analytics.

Once Kapler had been hired, he had voluntarily climbed into the mandibles of the Philadelphia sports scene without hesitation. While a coconut-scented breeze gently wafted through the palm trees of his former home in Malibu, Philadelphia was being thrashed by ice storms that filled the air with knives and left behind rivers of slush, quickly defiled by the city's boot prints and dog leavings. Kapler moved right in, and could be found lingering outside locally sourced restaurants in Northern Liberties and Fishtown, Apple products in hand, for most of the winter. As part of his introductory tour, Kapler, too, had gotten to attend a Sixers game and take part in the pregame bell-ringing ritual, doing so with an aggressive hammer strike that drew satisfied roars from the assembled sports fans.

By the Phillies' home opener, they were boos. He became the face the Phillies had sought for their franchise, but not in the way they had wanted.

"No, no!" the Phillies tried shouting over the boos. "Not him! Focus on *this* one!" they cried, desperately pointing at Rhys Hoskins stretching in the on-deck circle.

We don't have to relive the whole thing to understand what happened. Rather, there are three moments that do a pretty good job of painting the picture of Kapler's first year.

- **March 31:** With fans still heated over Kapler prematurely removing Aaron Nola from his opening day start and triggering a gut-punching loss, Kapler tries to bring reliever Hoby Milner into the game before the pitcher has warmed up in the bullpen. This leads to an uproar from players, analysts, umpires, and fans, who now have definitive proof that Kapler is the baseball antichrist. It was very clear very early that Kapler was not the kind of manager fans were used to seeing, and he was playing a kind of baseball they might not want to see. He also may not have fully understood the rules.
- **May 26:** Nola gives the Phillies six and two thirds of his best stuff, Maikel Franco crushes a deep line drive, and Nick Williams breaks a 1-1 tie in the eighth with a solo shot. The Phillies hold back the Blue Jays for a 2-1 win and slide into first place for the first time in seven years. They weren't there long, just a day, and only by a half-game margin. But it was enough that, after the Braves climbed back over the Phillies the next night, people wanted it back.
- **September 9:** Kapler says his team is in a "really good spot to strike," twitching the nose hairs of anyone who had just watched the downward spiraling Phillies lose four of six on a crucial road trip, further scattering their once promising playoff chances. Kapler has come under fire not just for the losing, but for the relentless positivity with which he chooses to face each downfall. If the Phillies were planning on striking, they did not do so, and lost 20 of 28 games in the regular season's final month.

There was a philosophical shift going on for the Phillies in 2018. The front office was focusing on accruing players who could take control of the strike zone, allowing for a deep pool of on-base threats from which Kapler, a strong advocate of these analytics himself, could select the best in-game matchups. Experimenting with this process, while also determining which young players were skilled enough for full-time jobs with the team—as well as determining what exactly a "full-time job" *meant* on this team—led to a clunky first season with Kapler at the helm. His management style, in which he employed such measures while refusing to denigrate his players in public and claimed to remain open to new ideas, drew the fire of rabid traditionalists, smirking columnists, and talking heads looking for a polarizing target.

And Kapler took them for a ride. This was a developmental season for the Phillies, so parts of it were always going to be a mess. The problem was, by reaching first place, his Phillies briefly became something else, as well: Contenders.

Philadelphia Phillies 2019

You could find fault with his methods, but with a first place team, you couldn't argue with Kapler's results (people *did*, though—just because the Phillies were changing doesn't mean Philadelphia was).

An 80-win team in Philadelphia was quite the quantifiable improvement, compared to their 66-win squad of the previous year (more commonly known as a "96-loss" squad). And your typical 80-win team is going to climb and stumble without every getting too far from the ground: a good month here, a bad stretch there, a power surge, a team-wide slump, somebody forgets to check the expiration date on post-game spread, etc. If the Phillies had lost their 82 games proportionally throughout the season, this page you're reading would be covered in an essay about how the Phillies laid a foundation from which they can build. Instead, they won in clumps, lost in batches, and played themselves right into and out of the contention that had caught everyone by pleasant surprise.

Kapler being a rookie himself played into this. His belief in the numbers cost him on a few occasions, trusting them over what he could see with his eyes when it came to relievers. His lineup was never the same twice, and the front office seemed convinced they could turn Kingery into Ben Zobrist just by writing new positions next to his name. They wanted so badly to be a team of 25 super utility on-base machines, taking pitches and slapping singles, but they just didn't have the tools for it. One of their two big off-season acquisitions, Carlos Santana, embodied this perfectly: A veteran player brought in to duplicate the role already filled by the team's face, Hoskins. A solid idea, bringing in one of the best players in the league at getting on base, and at a reasonable rate, but without an established bat in the lineup to knock him in, all he could do was stand out there.

In the clubhouse, there was no one for Kapler to rely on. He had Nola, the sole All-Star, a steadfast presence on the roster for the entire season. He had Hoskins, who was ready to be crowned the leader in the locker room but didn't quite have his own swing figured out and was still playing in his first full big league season. He had Santana, who just wasn't the type of player the Phillies needed, he had Jake Arrieta, whose patience wore thin, as did veteran Pat Neshek's. Beyond that, Kapler's roster was full of young players trying to rise to the occasion but kept bonking their heads on low ceilings.

The Phillies fell into an identity crisis. They looked in the mirror every morning and saw, what, exactly? A rebuilding team? A developing team? A National League contender? Carlos Santana playing shortstop in one of Kapler's shifts?

A team that improves by 14 wins gets to ask itself, "How do we build from this?"

A team that falls out of playoff contention over the season's last eight weeks has to answer… other questions. And one of them is, "Where did this team go?"

If development is about finding out what you have, then the Phillies found out plenty in 2018: Chiefly, that there *is* talent on this team, but plenty of room for more. The talent they do have could use support in order to be sustained through a full 162-game slog. True progress, as it occurs, can be hard to watch, and nobody was harder to watch in the second half of 2018 than the Phillies. Their failures were amplified by their earlier success, and as the team cratered come September, it left a lot of people wondering: In a development year, is it *possible* to fail? Or do you just learn things you didn't want to know?

The Phillies sealed themselves off, letting little information about their future plans squeak out. This follows a trend started by a 2017 preseason incident involving a "sensitivity bus" in the clubhouse that created a stir and Kapler squelched without incident. Throughout the season, Kapler delivered robust, flowery monologues after games and GM Matt Klentak gave empty, diplomatic responses during infrequent appearances, both of which explained nothing. Combined with the team's lackluster performances, it created a frustration among fans, amplified by the team's early season success and ultimate deflation. We've now latched onto Middleton's comment that he would "even be a little bit stupid about" spending money to improve the team, and created a world in which the Phillies are a failure in 2019 if they don't build a monstrosity so heavy with talent that it crushes both the NL East and the luxury tax threshold into dust.

"Losing streaks are funny," Gene Mauch, author of one of the least funny losing streaks of all time, once said. "If you lose at the beginning you got off to a bad start. If you lose in the middle of the season, you're in a slump. If you lose at the end, you're choking."

The 2018 Phillies, it was widely presumed, were always going to lose around 82 games. They just picked the wrong time to lose them.

Mauch also once said, "Baseball and malaria keep coming back." In the end, the Phillies finding the sort of persistence at the heart of both America's pastime and a mosquito-borne tropical disease will be what achieves them the relevance they seek. That, and the talented established players they can afford to acquire. Those will help. And with these attainable qualities, the Phillies can keep up with—and potentially outpace—the growing competitiveness of the NL East.

Along the way, they'll keep changing, keep failing, and keep learning from the failing. And if things really get hairy, they can always try switching the bullpens.

—*Justin Klugh is an author of Baseball Prospectus.*

Part 2: Player Analysis

Philadelphia Phillies 2019

Aaron Altherr OF

Born: 01/14/91 Age: 28 Bats: R Throws: R
Height: 6'5" Weight: 215 Origin: Round 9, 2009 Draft (#287 overall)

YEAR	TEAM	LVL	AGE	PA	R	2B	3B	HR	RBI	BB	K	SB	CS	AVG/OBP/SLG
2016	PHI	MLB	25	227	23	6	0	4	22	23	69	7	2	.197/.300/.288
2017	PHI	MLB	26	412	58	24	5	19	65	32	104	5	4	.272/.340/.516
2018	LEH	AAA	27	134	15	5	0	2	12	14	37	4	0	.244/.321/.336
2018	PHI	MLB	27	285	28	11	1	8	38	36	91	3	2	.181/.295/.333
2019	PHI	MLB	28	187	22	8	1	6	21	18	52	3	1	.236/.321/.406

Breakout: 3%   Improve: 38%   Collapse: 19%   Attrition: 34%   MLB: 81%
Comparables: Travis Buck, Gabe Gross, Brent Lillibridge

Altherr's kidnapping was an underreported story in 2018. Not a lot of media attention was paid to the case of a guy who had simply vanished, and the decoy put in his place was a poor imitation. I mean, sure, the doppelganger **looked** like Aaron Altherr, but this other fellow couldn't play baseball nearly as well. He had a huge spike in K rate, couldn't hit for nearly as much power, and took way more pitches (probably to try and limit the chances of exposing himself as a fake, the clever devil). The Phillies finally got wise to the ruse and optioned the impostor to Triple-A in late July, executed a covert black ops mission to find the original Altherr, and brought him back in September. How the club managed to miss the signs of Altherr's disappearance for so many months may forever remain an unsolved mystery, but they're probably just as happy as the rest of us to have seen the real thing finally find his way home after months of struggle.

YEAR	TEAM	LVL	AGE	PA	DRC+	VORP	BABIP	BRR	FRAA	WARP
2016	PHI	MLB	25	227	72	-0.7	.280	0.3	RF(42): -2.6, LF(20): 3.0	-0.2
2017	PHI	MLB	26	412	107	23.4	.328	0.4	LF(52): 4.3, RF(50): 1.6	2.2
2018	LEH	AAA	27	134	90	-0.2	.333	-0.6	CF(21): -0.6, LF(8): 2.7	0.2
2018	PHI	MLB	27	285	73	-5.0	.247	-1.2	RF(68): -4.2, CF(11): -0.4	-0.8
2019	PHI	MLB	28	187	92	4.6	.295	0.0	LF 1, CF 0	0.6

Aaron Altherr, continued

Batted Ball Distribution

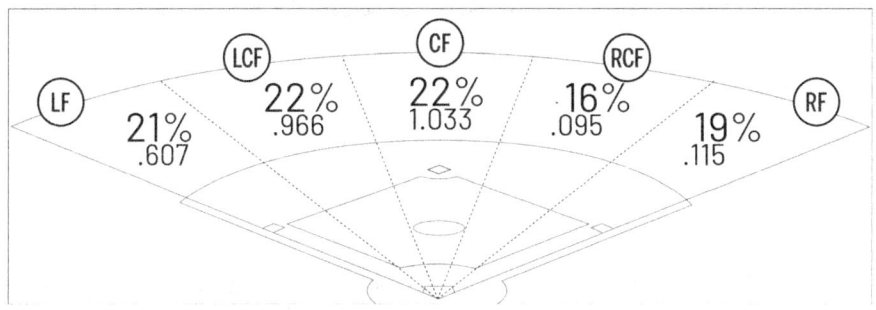

Strike Zone vs LHP   Strike Zone vs RHP

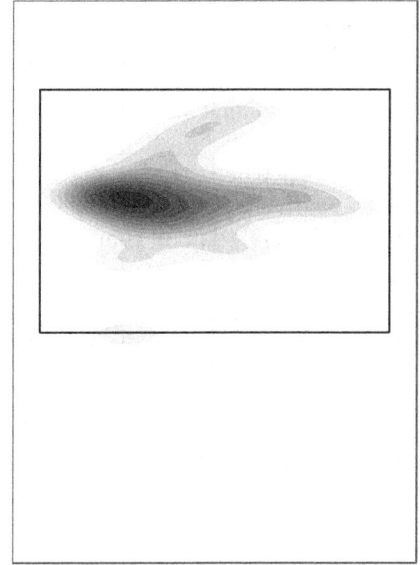
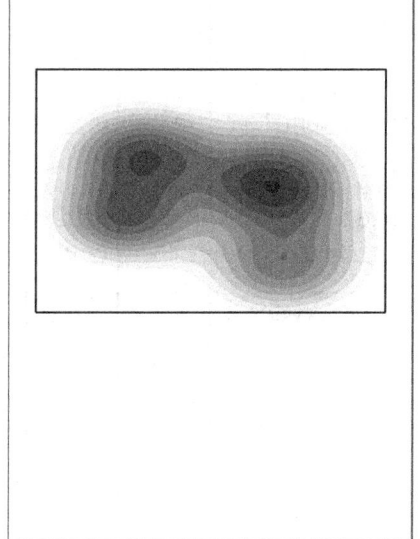

Drew Butera C

Born: 08/09/83 Age: 35 Bats: R Throws: R
Height: 6'1" Weight: 205 Origin: Round 5, 2005 Draft (#149 overall)

YEAR	TEAM	LVL	AGE	PA	R	2B	3B	HR	RBI	BB	K	SB	CS	AVG/OBP/SLG
2016	KCA	MLB	32	133	18	10	1	4	16	8	36	0	0	.285/.328/.480
2017	KCA	MLB	33	177	18	4	1	3	14	12	41	0	0	.227/.284/.319
2018	KCA	MLB	34	166	11	9	0	2	18	13	37	0	0	.188/.259/.289
2018	COL	MLB	34	16	2	0	0	1	3	2	2	0	0	.214/.313/.429
2019	PHI	MLB	35	63	6	3	0	1	6	5	15	0	0	.228/.302/.333

Breakout: 5% Improve: 31% Collapse: 14% Attrition: 35% MLB: 86%
Comparables: Mike Matheny, Gus Mancuso, Ivey Wingo

"Failing upwards" isn't quite the correct turn of phrase, but anyone who's managed to post only three positive-WARP seasons this decade and still hang on to a big-league roster spot deserves our praise and admiration. Butera got right to work on making sure that number didn't rise in 2018, with a further slide in defensive efficiency joining his regular parades from dugout to dish and right back again. And somehow Kansas City managed to get a semi-interesting relief prospect back when they found a willing trade partner for him in Colorado at the end of August. Now 35 and buried among a deep free-agent class of catchers, Butera's days of guaranteed contractual cover may finally be at an end.

YEAR	TEAM	P. COUNT	FRM RUNS	BLK RUNS	THRW RUNS	TOT RUNS
2016	KCA	5369	1.8	-0.4	-0.1	1.0
2017	KCA	7350	-4.2	2.0	-0.2	-3.0
2018	KCA	6521	-6.4	0.0	-0.2	-6.8
2018	COL	730	-0.7	-0.1	0.0	-0.9
2019	PHI	2570	-1.8	0.2	-0.1	-1.8

YEAR	TEAM	LVL	AGE	PA	DRC+	VORP	BABIP	BRR	FRAA	WARP
2016	KCA	MLB	32	133	87	6.0	.373	-1.1	C(51): 0.5, 1B(2): 0.0	0.4
2017	KCA	MLB	33	177	84	1.2	.286	-0.1	C(74): -3.4, 1B(4): -0.2	0.2
2018	KCA	MLB	34	166	80	-0.4	.232	1.2	C(48): -6.9, 1B(2): 0.9	-0.1
2018	COL	MLB	34	16	78	0.5	.182	0.1	C(6): -0.9, 1B(4): 0.0	-0.1
2019	PHI	MLB	35	63	75	1.0	.298	-0.1	C -2	-0.2

Drew Butera, continued

Batted Ball Distribution

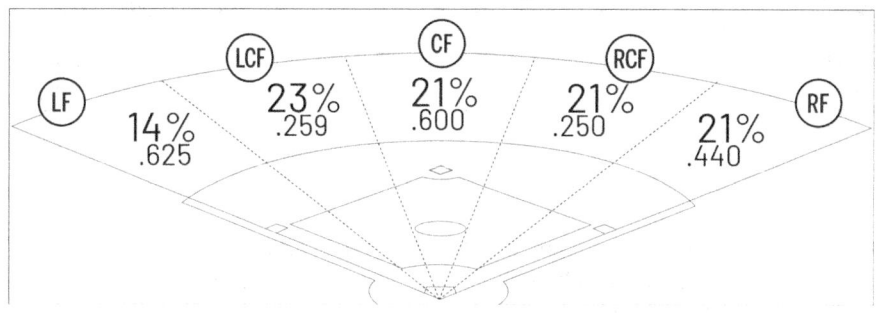

Strike Zone vs LHP

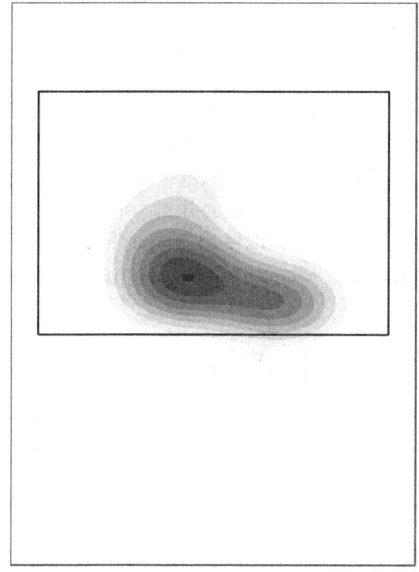

Strike Zone vs RHP

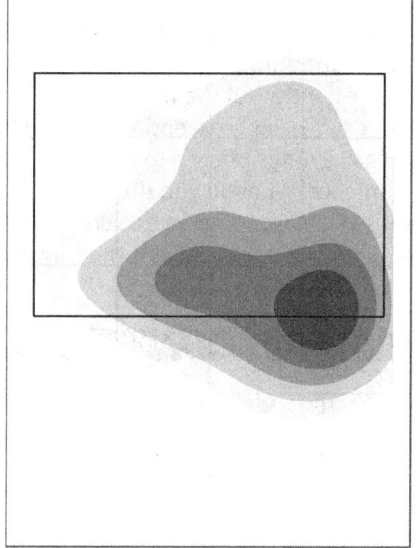

Maikel Franco 3B
Born: 08/26/92 Age: 26 Bats: R Throws: R
Height: 6'1" Weight: 215 Origin: International Free Agent, 2010

YEAR	TEAM	LVL	AGE	PA	R	2B	3B	HR	RBI	BB	K	SB	CS	AVG/OBP/SLG
2016	PHI	MLB	23	630	67	23	1	25	88	40	106	1	1	.255/.306/.427
2017	PHI	MLB	24	623	66	29	1	24	76	41	95	0	0	.230/.281/.409
2018	PHI	MLB	25	465	48	17	1	22	68	29	62	1	0	.270/.314/.467
2019	PHI	MLB	26	501	57	22	2	18	64	38	78	1	0	.253/.313/.428

Breakout: 7% Improve: 56% Collapse: 4% Attrition: 9% MLB: 93%
Comparables: Wilmer Flores, Matt Duffy, Kyle Seager

Fans have now spent three years awaiting the return of the 2015 version of Franco. The then-22-year-old's excellent half-season has never been replicated, much to the chagrin of those not content to continue waiting to see if roster lottery tickets can be cashed in, but 2018 provided the closest imitation and brightest glimmer of hope for an eventual reprisal. Franco, still just 26, was having a better season than his final line suggests, hitting .281/.321/.490 as late as August 22 before losing time to a wrist injury and, shortly thereafter, neck and shoulder problems sustained from a fall into a camera well. He still possesses the arm for third base, and an above-average hitter is by no means a **bad** thing to have handy. But the flaws of sub-par pitch recognition—saved only by a rather surprisingly exceptional ability to make contact—and lead-footed defensive range offset a lot of his offensive value, even in the face of a potential resurgence. What do you do with a player like that? A move to first subtracts his arm's value, and a move to a corner outfield spot does little to help a team beset by defensive issues. Such is the tragedy of players with plenty of talent, none of it supernatural.

YEAR	TEAM	LVL	AGE	PA	DRC+	VORP	BABIP	BRR	FRAA	WARP
2016	PHI	MLB	23	630	102	23.3	.271	-1.6	3B(148): -7.2	1.4
2017	PHI	MLB	24	623	82	2.2	.234	-1.8	3B(144): -9.2, 1B(2): -0.1	-0.3
2018	PHI	MLB	25	465	109	21.7	.270	1.5	3B(117): -2.7	2.1
2019	PHI	MLB	26	501	100	12.6	.268	-0.8	3B -7	0.4

Maikel Franco, continued

Batted Ball Distribution

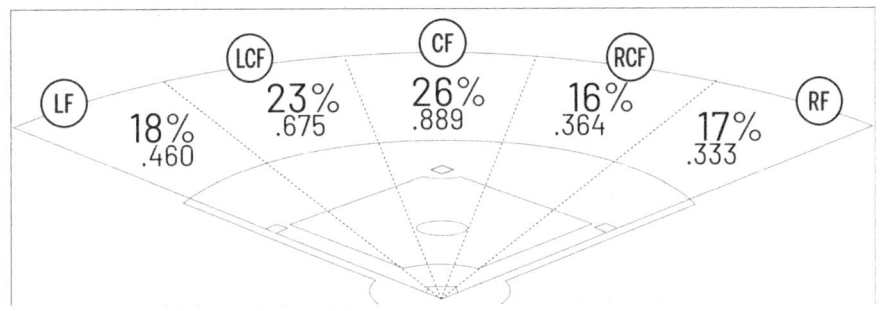

Strike Zone vs LHP

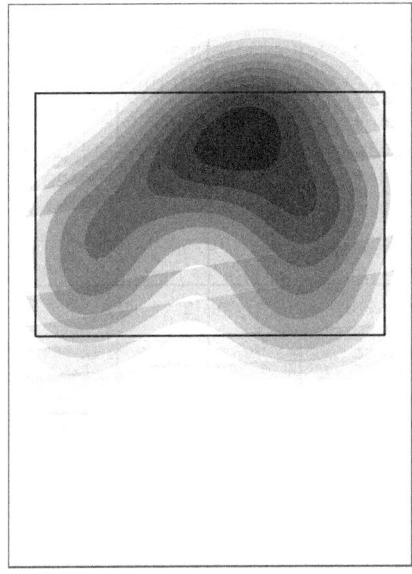

Strike Zone vs RHP

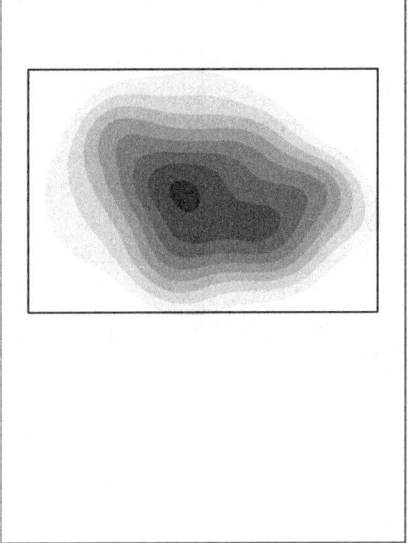

Bryce Harper OF

Born: 10/16/92   Age: 26   Bats: L   Throws: R
Height: 6'3"   Weight: 220   Origin: Round 1, 2010 Draft (#1 overall)

YEAR	TEAM	LVL	AGE	PA	R	2B	3B	HR	RBI	BB	K	SB	CS	AVG/OBP/SLG
2016	WAS	MLB	23	627	84	24	2	24	86	108	117	21	10	.243/.373/.441
2017	WAS	MLB	24	492	95	27	1	29	87	68	99	4	2	.319/.413/.595
2018	WAS	MLB	25	695	103	34	0	34	100	130	169	13	3	.249/.393/.496
2019	PHI	MLB	26	615	89	29	2	28	89	93	143	11	4	.269/.384/.497

Breakout: 2%   Improve: 51%   Collapse: 6%   Attrition: 3%   MLB: 100%
Comparables: Mel Ott, Frank Robinson, Frank Thomas

The most ballyhooed amateur baseball player in recent memory, Harper was simultaneously and surreptitiously cast as the antagonist in a billion personal hero movies. Cole Hamels' righteous plunking (which resulted in the glorious steal of home). Jonathan Papelbon's turn as a raging TV cop in an interrogation room. The Statcast-enlightened internet's intellectual thriller in which his 2015 is a partial sham. The anonymous scout's tick-tock rush to expose a double-agent-style impostor who lacks the grit to win. Hunter Strickland's turn as a version of Liam Neeson who relies only on coincidental meetings. Even in his Home Run Derby triumph, it was hard to look at Harper without thinking of Johnny Lawrence and the Cobra Kai. He was appointed huge-contract A-Rod without the money or the villainy. Now, Harper has reached the huge contract portion of his career, and will remain that boogeyman to many. His outsized personality, however, is a bankable vehicle for baseball, regardless of the storylines' origin. Everyone is in his movie, whether they know it or not, and moving simply further up I-95 to a division rival will only serve up some additional heated dialogue during the many summers to come.

YEAR	TEAM	LVL	AGE	PA	DRC+	VORP	BABIP	BRR	FRAA	WARP
2016	WAS	MLB	23	627	118	42.1	.264	2.3	RF(143): 4.1	3.4
2017	WAS	MLB	24	492	147	47.0	.356	-1.3	RF(110): -3.4	3.5
2018	WAS	MLB	25	695	126	52.2	.289	-3.2	RF(116): -12.1, CF(63): -0.1	2.5
2019	PHI	MLB	26	615	137	45.3	.320	-0.1	RF -9	3.6

Bryce Harper, continued

Batted Ball Distribution

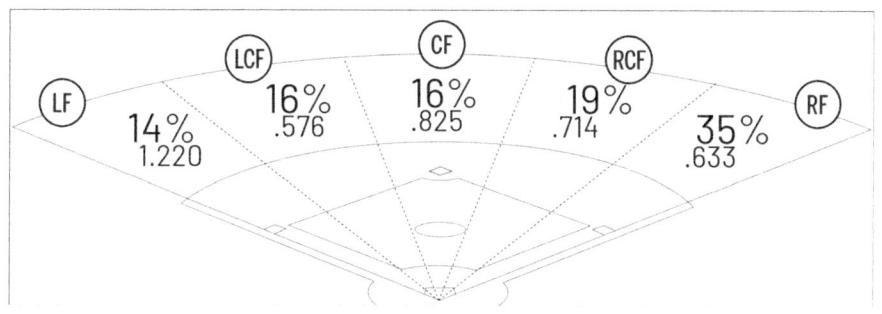

Strike Zone vs LHP

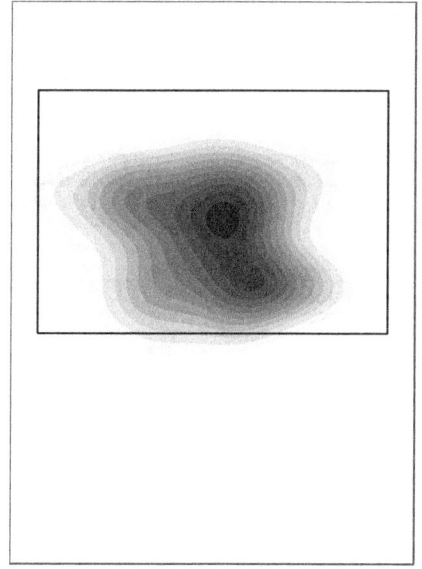

Strike Zone vs RHP

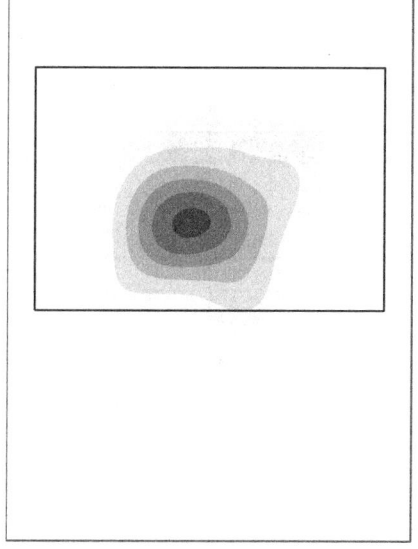

Cesar Hernandez 2B

Born: 05/23/90   Age: 29   Bats: B   Throws: R
Height: 5'10"   Weight: 160   Origin: International Free Agent, 2006

YEAR	TEAM	LVL	AGE	PA	R	2B	3B	HR	RBI	BB	K	SB	CS	AVG/OBP/SLG
2016	PHI	MLB	26	622	67	14	11	6	39	66	116	17	13	.294/.371/.393
2017	PHI	MLB	27	577	85	26	6	9	34	61	104	15	5	.294/.373/.421
2018	PHI	MLB	28	708	91	15	3	15	60	95	155	19	6	.253/.356/.362
2019	PHI	MLB	29	594	78	22	4	12	55	64	124	15	6	.272/.355/.399

Breakout: 2%   Improve: 48%   Collapse: 9%   Attrition: 7%   MLB: 99%
Comparables: Craig Biggio, Eddie Moore, Buddy Myer

What happens when a player enters a season among the most underrated in the league and exits it with a step back in nearly every offensive category—save for home runs, weirdly enough—and a whole lot of roster redundancy staring him down? After steady improvement from 2015-17, Cesar seemed like a guy who'd enter his age 28 season ready to lock 'n' load. In the first half, things mostly went according to plan until, like a lot of other players on this Philly roster, the entire thing fell apart for some reason. Some surmise Hernandez played the latter half of the year on a bum foot after fouling a pitch off it, but whatever the cause, a .657 post-All-Star OPS can't quite be the star turn the Phillies might have hoped for.

YEAR	TEAM	LVL	AGE	PA	DRC+	VORP	BABIP	BRR	FRAA	WARP
2016	PHI	MLB	26	622	98	33.4	.363	-0.9	2B(149): -0.4, SS(4): -0.2	1.6
2017	PHI	MLB	27	577	103	37.3	.353	4.2	2B(127): -2.4, SS(1): 0.0	2.2
2018	PHI	MLB	28	708	101	30.1	.315	2.0	2B(154): 3.7	2.9
2019	PHI	MLB	29	594	103	25.5	.331	0.6	2B -1	2.3

Cesar Hernandez, continued

Batted Ball Distribution

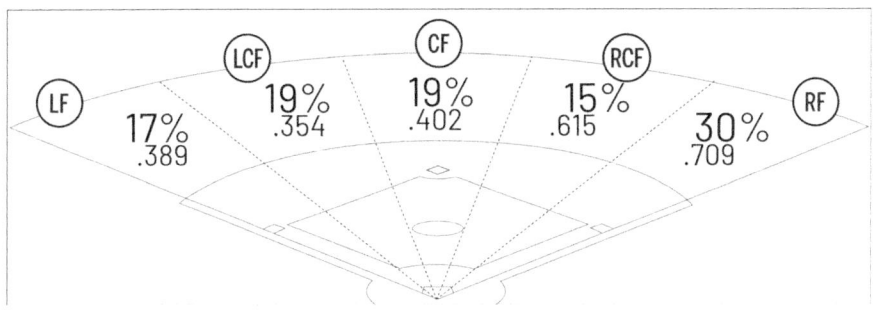

Strike Zone vs LHP

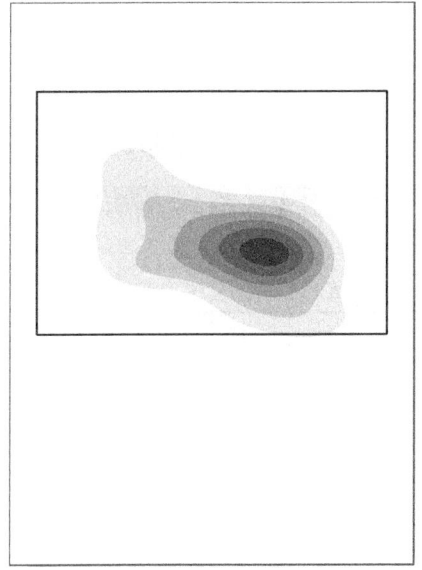

Strike Zone vs RHP

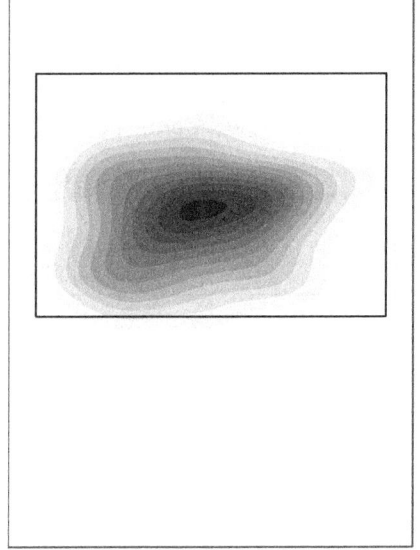

Odubel Herrera CF

Born: 12/29/91 Age: 27 Bats: L Throws: R
Height: 5'11" Weight: 205 Origin: International Free Agent, 2008

YEAR	TEAM	LVL	AGE	PA	R	2B	3B	HR	RBI	BB	K	SB	CS	AVG/OBP/SLG
2016	PHI	MLB	24	656	87	21	6	15	49	63	134	25	7	.286/.361/.420
2017	PHI	MLB	25	563	67	42	3	14	56	31	126	8	5	.281/.325/.452
2018	PHI	MLB	26	597	64	19	3	22	71	38	122	5	2	.255/.310/.420
2019	PHI	MLB	27	449	55	21	3	13	51	33	96	8	3	.269/.330/.430

Breakout: 6%   Improve: 51%   Collapse: 9%   Attrition: 7%   MLB: 97%
Comparables: Mickey Brantley, Carl Furillo, Amos Otis

If one single player could embody all of the characteristics needed to bifurcate an entire fan base, well, you're reading about him. Herrera exists at the crossroads between Fun Street, Potential Avenue, Infuriating Boulevard, and Unique Lane, the four main thoroughfares of the planet he inhabits. For the first three years of his career, it was easier to soothe the nerves of everyone frustrated by his mercurial play by pointing to the overall numbers and saying "Hey, look, this isn't so bad!" When the ability to make that argument evaporates in the wake of a .215/.265/.368 stretch from May 22 on, it becomes tougher to keep the sports radio hosts at bay. There's plenty of talent contained in this alien's body, but if his downward trend continues on into 2019, more folks might start wondering how long it'd take to fuel his spaceship up.

YEAR	TEAM	LVL	AGE	PA	DRC+	VORP	BABIP	BRR	FRAA	WARP
2016	PHI	MLB	24	656	104	45.7	.349	3.1	CF(155): 8.3	3.7
2017	PHI	MLB	25	563	90	22.7	.345	-1.8	CF(133): 10.5	2.1
2018	PHI	MLB	26	597	93	20.8	.290	0.8	CF(133): -1.1, RF(9): -1.2	1.4
2019	PHI	MLB	27	449	101	18.5	.321	0.1	CF 1, LF 0	1.8

Odubel Herrera, continued

Batted Ball Distribution

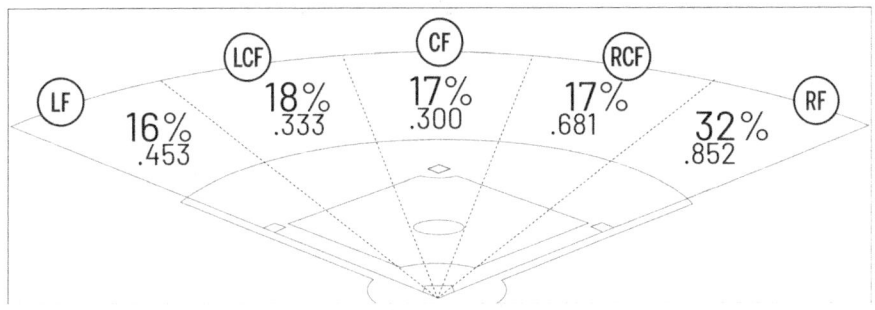

Strike Zone vs LHP   Strike Zone vs RHP

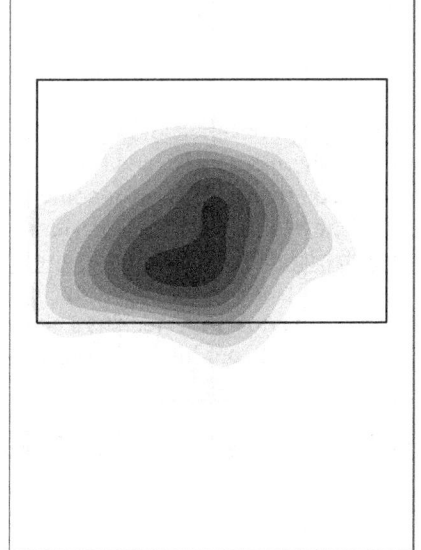

Rhys Hoskins LF

Born: 03/17/93 Age: 26 Bats: R Throws: R
Height: 6'4" Weight: 225 Origin: Round 5, 2014 Draft (#142 overall)

YEAR	TEAM	LVL	AGE	PA	R	2B	3B	HR	RBI	BB	K	SB	CS	AVG/OBP/SLG
2016	REA	AA	23	589	95	26	1	38	116	71	125	8	3	.281/.377/.566
2017	LEH	AAA	24	475	78	24	4	29	91	64	75	4	2	.284/.385/.581
2017	PHI	MLB	24	212	37	7	0	18	48	37	46	2	0	.259/.396/.618
2018	PHI	MLB	25	660	89	38	0	34	96	87	150	5	3	.246/.354/.496
2019	PHI	MLB	26	623	92	30	2	29	82	79	134	4	2	.244/.348/.472

Breakout: 1% Improve: 55% Collapse: 8% Attrition: 6% MLB: 98%
Comparables: Matt Joyce, Derek Dietrich, Corey Dickerson

Hoskins has played a lot of baseball these last two years. This past season, the only games he missed were the nine he was forced to miss immediately after breaking his jaw on a foul ball, and he rather promptly made up for it by flying to Japan to take part in the six-game Japan Series exhibition in November. In 2017, between the Majors and minors, Hoskins played in a combined **165** games. It's a testament to his durability that Hoskins didn't really show signs of wear and tear or fatigue at the end of either marathon season, though '18 did contain a handful of cold streaks sprinkled throughout. And while 2018 seemed to position him more as the next Pat Burrell than Paul Goldschmidt, we've all evolved in our baseball knowledge enough to understand that any player who falls anywhere between those two endpoints provides plenty of offensive value. Defense, on the other hand, is something of a problem. It certainly would've made Matt Klentak's job a bit easier if Hoskins had adapted to left field the way the club hoped he would entering the year, but...well, he didn't, and the Phillies were left with a glut of corner-only players who couldn't handle the corners. It's a comfort to know that Hoskins's bat will play in any lineup, no matter where his glove gets stuck, but his pitchers are likely to appreciate him more now that his home is at first base.

YEAR	TEAM	LVL	AGE	PA	DRC+	VORP	BABIP	BRR	FRAA	WARP
2016	REA	AA	23	589	140	38.2	.297	-1.1	1B(129): -0.6	1.9
2017	LEH	AAA	24	475	157	37.6	.281	-0.6	1B(105): -9.8, LF(3): 0.2	1.8
2017	PHI	MLB	24	212	151	27.4	.241	-0.1	LF(30): -0.8, 1B(27): -0.3	1.6
2018	PHI	MLB	25	660	129	47.4	.272	0.2	LF(135): -0.7, 1B(17): 0.2	3.9
2019	PHI	MLB	26	623	121	29.0	.271	-0.9	1B -4	2.5

Rhys Hoskins, continued

Batted Ball Distribution

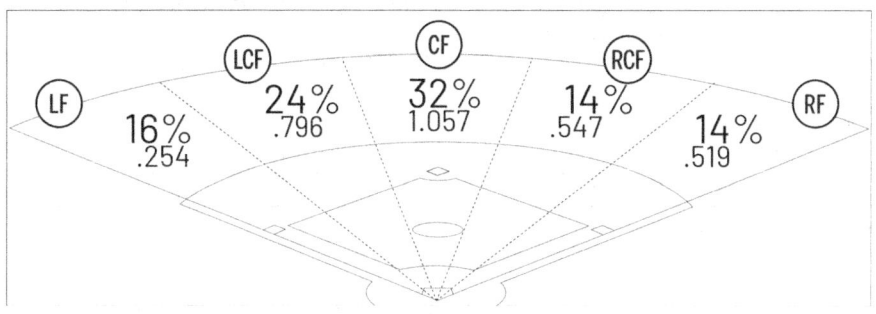

Strike Zone vs LHP

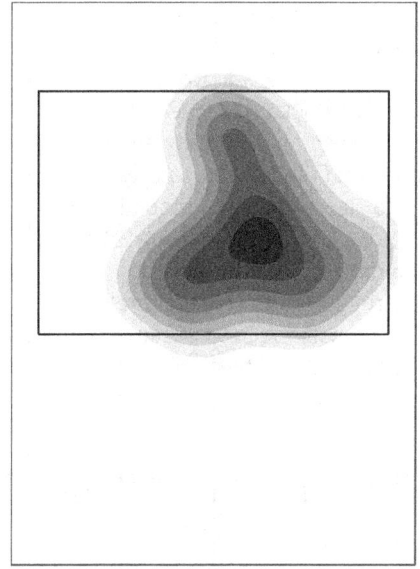

Strike Zone vs RHP

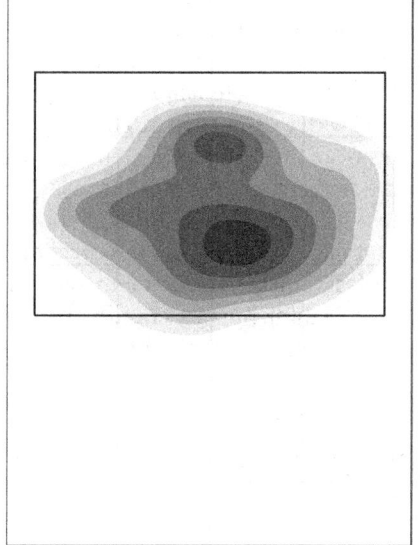

Scott Kingery SS

Born: 04/29/94 Age: 25 Bats: R Throws: R
Height: 5'10" Weight: 180 Origin: Round 2, 2015 Draft (#48 overall)

YEAR	TEAM	LVL	AGE	PA	R	2B	3B	HR	RBI	BB	K	SB	CS	AVG/OBP/SLG
2016	CLR	A+	22	420	60	29	3	3	28	33	54	26	5	.293/.360/.411
2016	REA	AA	22	166	16	7	0	2	18	5	36	4	2	.250/.273/.333
2017	REA	AA	23	317	62	18	5	18	44	28	51	19	3	.313/.379/.608
2017	LEH	AAA	23	286	41	11	3	8	21	13	58	10	2	.294/.337/.449
2018	PHI	MLB	24	484	55	23	2	8	35	24	126	10	3	.226/.267/.338
2019	PHI	MLB	25	410	45	16	2	10	39	23	102	11	3	.233/.282/.365

Breakout: 11% Improve: 60% Collapse: 9% Attrition: 41% MLB: 92%
Comparables: Eduardo Nunez, Brandon Crawford, Cory Spangenberg

There were risks. There were reasons to be skeptical. There were causes for caution. Presumably cognizant of them all, the Phillies gave Scott Kingery a six-year Major League deal before he'd played a single MLB game, and he responded by having one of the worst offensive performances of any regular in the league. Kingery grabbed the attention of the greater Philadelphia area thanks to a scorching-hot half-season in Double-A in 2017 and little else; he'd dropped a .606 OPS in 37 games at the same level just a year prior. It's hard enough adjusting to Major League pitching on its own, but Kingery was also tasked with learning how to be the everyday shortstop on-the-fly and on the heels of an attempt to play him at third base that failed spectacularly. Kingery was adequate at short, thanks in large part to clearly being a gifted athlete whose range was up to the challenge but whose arm clearly belongs at second. Everything about Kingery's 2018 felt forced: the contract, the position, the steadfast refusal to option him even as his struggles deepened. There's no reason to think Kingery couldn't be an elite defensive second baseman given his athletic toolset, and he'd be put in a position to succeed by playing there regularly, but he and incumbent Cesar Hernandez will have to coexist for another season.

YEAR	TEAM	LVL	AGE	PA	DRC+	VORP	BABIP	BRR	FRAA	WARP
2016	CLR	A+	22	420	140	26.0	.334	1.6	2B(88): 7.7	2.9
2016	REA	AA	22	166	62	-0.6	.306	1.9	2B(37): -1.4	-0.4
2017	REA	AA	23	317	148	35.0	.324	2.7	2B(59): 1.7	2.3
2017	LEH	AAA	23	286	109	10.2	.348	-1.2	2B(54): 0.9, 3B(4): 0.3	0.8
2018	PHI	MLB	24	484	70	4.3	.291	2.1	SS(119): -3.9, 3B(10): -0.2	0.2
2019	PHI	MLB	25	410	69	-0.2	.290	1.2	2B 1, 3B -1	-0.1

Scott Kingery, continued

Batted Ball Distribution

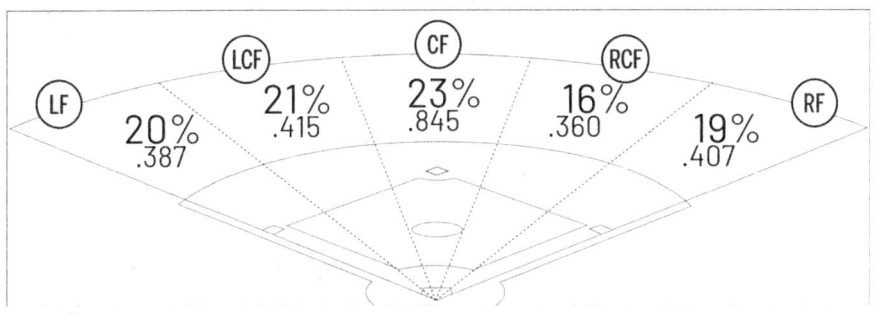

Strike Zone vs LHP   **Strike Zone vs RHP**

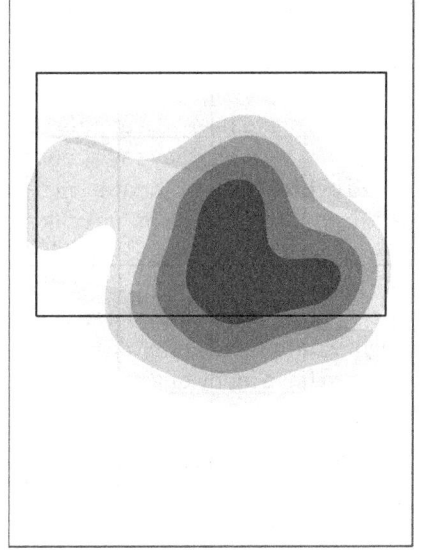

Andrew Knapp C

Born: 11/09/91 Age: 27 Bats: B Throws: R
Height: 6'1" Weight: 195 Origin: Round 2, 2013 Draft (#53 overall)

YEAR	TEAM	LVL	AGE	PA	R	2B	3B	HR	RBI	BB	K	SB	CS	AVG/OBP/SLG
2016	LEH	AAA	24	443	55	24	1	8	46	37	107	2	2	.266/.330/.390
2017	PHI	MLB	25	204	26	8	1	3	13	31	56	1	0	.257/.368/.368
2018	LEH	AAA	26	25	2	1	0	0	1	5	6	0	0	.250/.400/.300
2018	PHI	MLB	26	215	19	6	2	4	15	24	75	1	0	.198/.294/.316
2019	PHI	MLB	27	161	17	7	1	4	17	16	46	1	0	.239/.319/.387

Breakout: 5% Improve: 47% Collapse: 13% Attrition: 23% MLB: 87%
Comparables: Martin Maldonado, Hank Conger, JD Closser

If you squint or tilt your head just right while looking at Knapp's 2017 numbers, you could almost start to see a silhouette of early Stephen Vogt appear out of the negative space like some sort of apparition. Here was a

YEAR	TEAM	P. COUNT	FRM RUNS	BLK RUNS	THRW RUNS	TOT RUNS
2017	PHI	7630	-6.1	-1.6	-1.2	-8.8
2018	PHI	6630	-3.5	-0.4	-0.3	-4.3
2019	PHI	3700	-1.7	-0.5	-0.1	-2.3

catcher by title—if not in proficiency—who could work a count, keep the strikeout totals manageable, and even provide a hint of pop. With a little luck, you'd think, that Vogt Ghost could become a little more corporeal in 2018, and the Phillies could have a neat little contingency in their back pocket for 2018. Well, you know what they say about the best-laid plans of Phanatics and men. Instead of breaking out, Knapp fell backward in nearly every aspect of his game: His strikeout rate soared as his walk rate plummeted, he whiffed more, and his FRAA ranked 99th among 117 qualified catchers. Given the Phillies' dearth of upper-level catching depth, Knapp was still the team's second-best catching option. But with a clear preference for cultivating Jorge Alfaro's game and an intriguing farmhand in Deivi Grullon waiting in the wings, don't expect the Phillies to have many qualms about seeking out an upgrade over Knapp for the backup backstop post.

YEAR	TEAM	LVL	AGE	PA	DRC+	VORP	BABIP	BRR	FRAA	WARP
2016	LEH	AAA	24	443	109	22.3	.343	0.9	C(104): 12.2, 1B(1): 0.0	3.3
2017	PHI	MLB	25	204	84	12.1	.360	0.1	C(53): -10.2, 1B(1): 0.0	-0.4
2018	LEH	AAA	26	25	113	1.3	.357	-0.2	C(4): 0.2, LF(1): -0.4	0.0
2018	PHI	MLB	26	215	68	5.6	.303	1.2	C(53): -5.4, 1B(1): 0.0	-0.3
2019	PHI	MLB	27	161	82	3.1	.312	-0.2	C -3, 1B 0	-0.1

Andrew Knapp, continued

Batted Ball Distribution

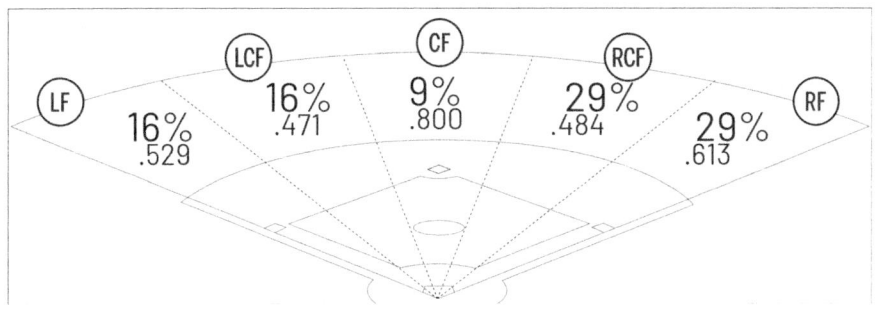

Strike Zone vs LHP

Strike Zone vs RHP

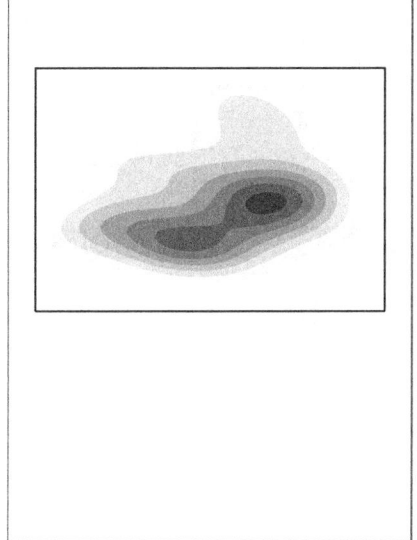

Andrew McCutchen RF

Born: 10/10/86 Age: 32 Bats: R Throws: R
Height: 5'11" Weight: 195 Origin: Round 1, 2005 Draft (#11 overall)

YEAR	TEAM	LVL	AGE	PA	R	2B	3B	HR	RBI	BB	K	SB	CS	AVG/OBP/SLG
2016	PIT	MLB	29	675	81	26	3	24	79	69	143	6	7	.256/.336/.430
2017	PIT	MLB	30	650	94	30	2	28	88	73	116	11	5	.279/.363/.486
2018	SFN	MLB	31	568	65	28	2	15	55	73	123	13	6	.255/.357/.415
2018	NYA	MLB	31	114	18	2	1	5	10	22	22	1	3	.253/.421/.471
2019	PHI	MLB	32	591	83	27	2	19	65	69	126	10	6	.259/.351/.431

Breakout: 0% Improve: 26% Collapse: 15% Attrition: 5% MLB: 97%
Comparables: Ben Zobrist, J.D. Drew, Milton Bradley

Andrew McCutchen and Giancarlo Stanton in the same Yankees outfield sounds like a 2013 Yankees fan message board fever dream, and yet here it was in 2018. Stanton is mostly the same player as then, but McCutchen most certainly is not, despite his usefulness in the Bronx. Necessitated by Aaron Judge's injury, Brian Cashman waited until the latest possible moment to both get his bat and minimize the bill, acquiring him on the last day before the trade waiver deadline. McCutchen rewarded the move with an .892 OPS in the month of September. If his short stint showed anything, it's that he is not going to fall off the map after becoming merely serviceable after his time in Pittsburgh. The defense will become completely untenable soon, but by hitting about 20% better than your average player, a team would be more than happy to take that trade-off in the short term.

YEAR	TEAM	LVL	AGE	PA	DRC+	VORP	BABIP	BRR	FRAA	WARP
2016	PIT	MLB	29	675	107	30.5	.297	-0.3	CF(151): -9.4	1.8
2017	PIT	MLB	30	650	124	50.0	.305	1.0	CF(139): -10.4, RF(13): -0.8	3.1
2018	SFN	MLB	31	568	116	22.3	.309	-3.7	RF(128): -4.9	1.4
2018	NYA	MLB	31	114	121	9.0	.279	0.3	RF(15): -1.9, LF(12): 0.0	0.4
2019	PHI	MLB	32	591	115	28.1	.309	-0.9	LF -1, RF -1	2.5

Andrew McCutchen, continued

Batted Ball Distribution

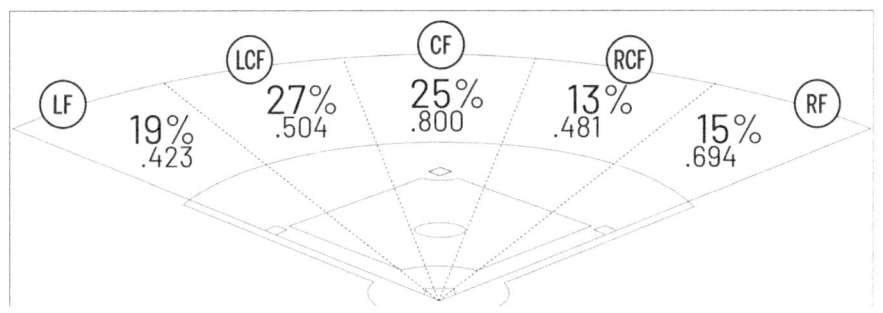

Strike Zone vs LHP

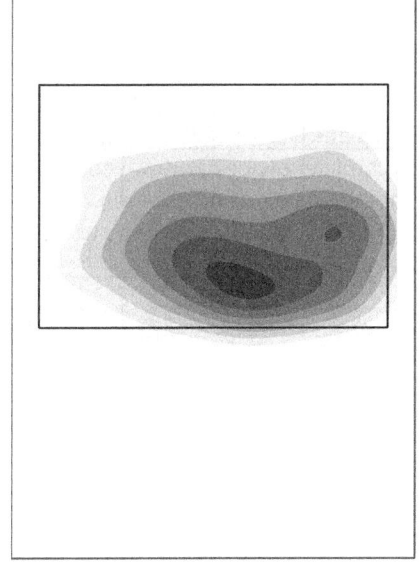

Strike Zone vs RHP

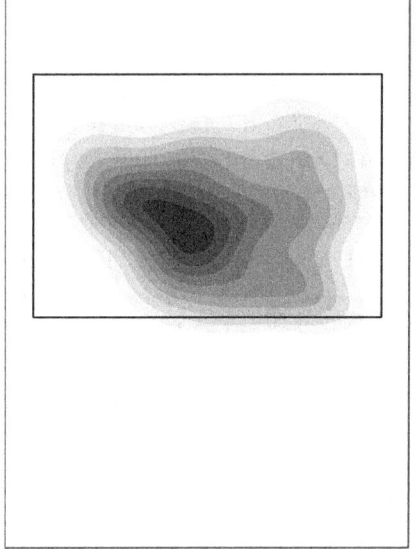

Roman Quinn CF

Born: 05/14/93 Age: 26 Bats: B Throws: R
Height: 5'10" Weight: 170 Origin: Round 2, 2011 Draft (#66 overall)

YEAR	TEAM	LVL	AGE	PA	R	2B	3B	HR	RBI	BB	K	SB	CS	AVG/OBP/SLG
2016	REA	AA	23	322	58	14	6	6	25	30	68	31	8	.287/.361/.441
2016	PHI	MLB	23	69	10	4	0	0	6	8	19	5	1	.263/.373/.333
2017	LEH	AAA	24	197	24	8	3	2	13	18	49	10	4	.274/.344/.389
2018	LEH	AAA	25	107	14	2	3	2	11	8	19	13	1	.296/.349/.439
2018	PHI	MLB	25	143	13	6	4	2	12	10	35	10	4	.260/.317/.412
2019	PHI	MLB	26	234	30	9	2	5	21	18	59	15	4	.237/.302/.370

Breakout: 7%   Improve: 41%   Collapse: 11%   Attrition: 26%   MLB: 74%
Comparables: James Jones, Abraham Almonte, Lorenzo Cain

For a hot minute, among the flurry of trades they made in July and August, it seemed like the Phillies' best acquisition was going to come from within. Quinn figuratively—and almost nearly literally—flew out of the gate, going 18-for-40 in the second half of August. He then hit .145 in September, and even though that cold spell somehow wasn't enough to quiet calls for his supplanting of incumbent center fielder Odubel Herrera, it certainly tempered thoughts of Quinn being a favorite to land a starting job in 2019. Assuming he can ever put his injury issues behind him, or at least catch up to and run alongside them, Quinn should provide a good deal of value as a quick switch-hitter without much of a platoon split. Those injury issues can't simply be hand-waved away, as they've limited him to fewer than 90 games in every one of his seven professional seasons, so the Phillies signed Andrew McCutchen, happy to spread out Quinn's playing time as the team's fourth outfielder.

YEAR	TEAM	LVL	AGE	PA	DRC+	VORP	BABIP	BRR	FRAA	WARP
2016	REA	AA	23	322	113	24.5	.357	9.6	CF(62): -6.6, LF(4): -0.8	1.7
2016	PHI	MLB	23	69	70	3.9	.395	0.8	LF(12): -0.1, RF(4): 0.1	0.1
2017	LEH	AAA	24	197	92	10.2	.368	3.8	CF(38): -0.4, LF(4): -0.2	0.5
2018	LEH	AAA	25	107	105	6.7	.351	3.5	CF(21): 0.3, RF(2): -0.2	0.6
2018	PHI	MLB	25	143	82	4.0	.340	-0.9	CF(30): 0.9, RF(5): 1.3	0.3
2019	PHI	MLB	26	234	79	3.3	.298	1.9	CF -1	0.4

Roman Quinn, continued

Batted Ball Distribution

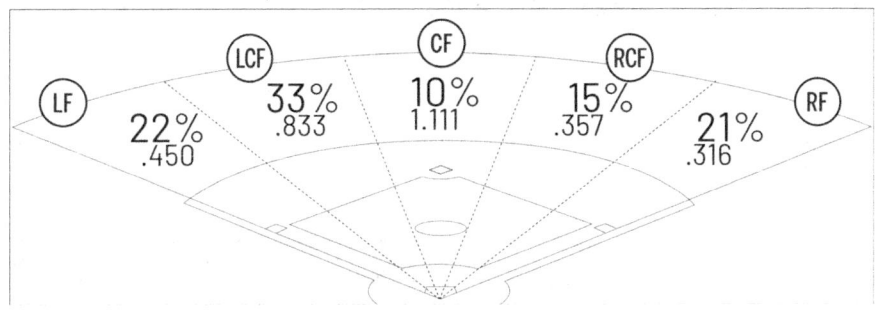

Strike Zone vs LHP   **Strike Zone vs RHP**

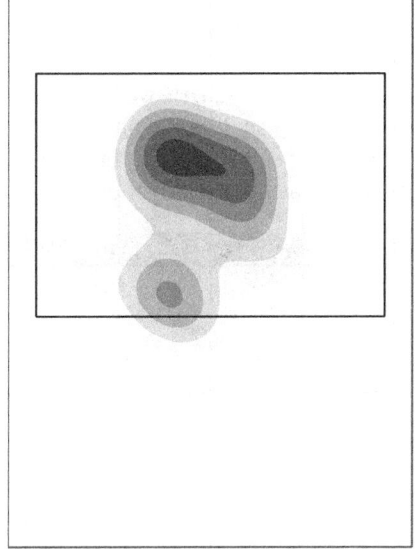

J.T. Realmuto C

Born: 03/18/91 Age: 28 Bats: R Throws: R
Height: 6'1" Weight: 210 Origin: Round 3, 2010 Draft (#104 overall)

YEAR	TEAM	LVL	AGE	PA	R	2B	3B	HR	RBI	BB	K	SB	CS	AVG/OBP/SLG
2016	MIA	MLB	25	545	60	31	0	11	48	28	100	12	4	.303/.343/.428
2017	MIA	MLB	26	579	68	31	5	17	65	36	106	8	2	.278/.332/.451
2018	MIA	MLB	27	531	74	30	3	21	74	38	104	3	2	.277/.340/.484
2019	PHI	MLB	28	551	66	28	3	18	69	39	107	7	3	.277/.338/.453

Breakout: 3% Improve: 40% Collapse: 19% Attrition: 12% MLB: 97%
Comparables: Jonathan Lucroy, Nick Hundley, Derek Norris

If 2017 was the year Realmuto announced his arrival to the baseball world, 2018 is the year he shouted to everyone that he's the best all-around catcher in the game. The 28-year-old generated value in a wide variety of ways. His traditional slash line categories ranked top two among catchers with a minimum of 400 plate appearances. He discovered newfound power after deciding to take to the skies with a new approach. He ranked as a plus defensively for the second straight season. He's also durable, one of just two catchers with at least 1,600 plate appearances since 2016. As the old guard of great catchers fades away, Realmuto has his grip firmly on the top spot.

YEAR	TEAM	P. COUNT	FRM RUNS	BLK RUNS	THRW RUNS	TOT RUNS
2016	MIA	18935	-8.5	1.8	2.1	-5.6
2017	MIA	18959	5.3	1.7	1.0	9.1
2018	MIA	16399	-0.4	0.9	0.1	0.4
2019	PHI	18448	-1.4	1.5	0.7	0.8

YEAR	TEAM	LVL	AGE	PA	DRC+	VORP	BABIP	BRR	FRAA	WARP
2016	MIA	MLB	25	545	103	38.0	.357	1.6	C(129): -0.1	3.0
2017	MIA	MLB	26	579	101	37.9	.318	1.0	C(126): 15.8, 1B(9): 0.3	4.5
2018	MIA	MLB	27	531	122	51.2	.312	4.1	C(112): 3.7, 1B(13): 0.6	4.8
2019	PHI	MLB	28	551	111	34.3	.321	-0.2	C 3, 1B 1	3.4

J.T. Realmuto, continued

Batted Ball Distribution

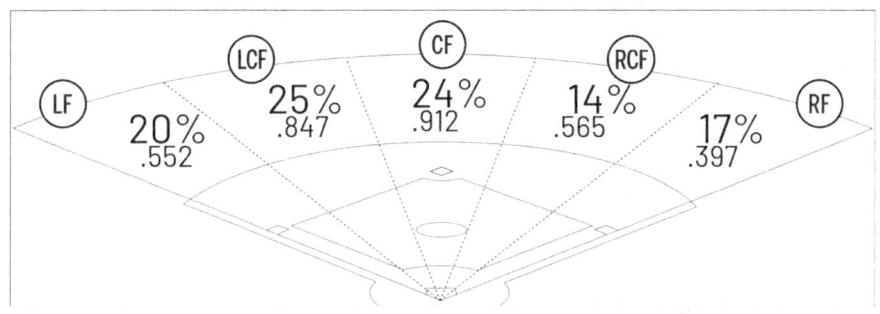

Strike Zone vs LHP

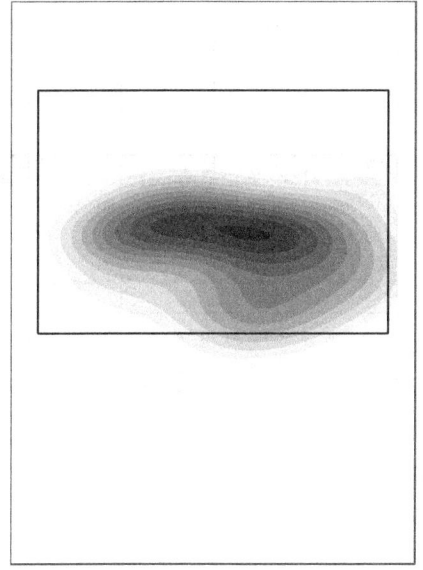

Strike Zone vs RHP

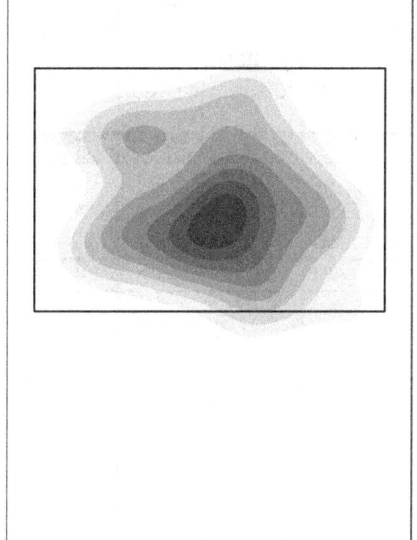

Jean Segura SS

Born: 03/17/90 Age: 29 Bats: R Throws: R
Height: 5'10" Weight: 205 Origin: International Free Agent, 2007

YEAR	TEAM	LVL	AGE	PA	R	2B	3B	HR	RBI	BB	K	SB	CS	AVG/OBP/SLG
2016	ARI	MLB	26	694	102	41	7	20	64	39	101	33	10	.319/.368/.499
2017	SEA	MLB	27	566	80	30	2	11	45	34	83	22	8	.300/.349/.427
2018	SEA	MLB	28	632	91	29	3	10	63	32	69	20	11	.304/.341/.415
2019	PHI	MLB	29	598	72	30	3	13	64	41	86	22	9	.289/.345/.426

Breakout: 3% Improve: 41% Collapse: 7% Attrition: 7% MLB: 100%
Comparables: Erick Aybar, Elvis Andrus, Rafael Furcal

Segura was good again in 2018. Really just quite good at playing shortstop, and hitting, and running around out there. He was just really good and absolutely not even a little bit better than that. It's possible that calling him a slightly above-average shortstop on a reasonable contract sounds like faint praise, but unless your team is blessed with a Lindor or a Correa, chances are Segura would be a big improvement over your in-house options. More than any other position on the diamond, perhaps, we tend to think of shortstop as wizards or failures, but for a Phillies fanbase, "fine" will feel awfully refreshing. At 29, his hit tool will carry him anywhere in the middle infield his team needs him for at least the foreseeable future. He's really just quite good.

YEAR	TEAM	LVL	AGE	PA	DRC+	VORP	BABIP	BRR	FRAA	WARP
2016	ARI	MLB	26	694	117	54.8	.353	6.5	2B(142): 5.3, SS(23): 0.2	4.9
2017	SEA	MLB	27	566	104	27.6	.339	2.1	SS(124): -8.9	2.2
2018	SEA	MLB	28	632	105	35.9	.327	-1.0	SS(144): 3.4	3.5
2019	PHI	MLB	29	598	106	30.6	.320	1.0	SS -3	2.6

Jean Segura, continued

Batted Ball Distribution

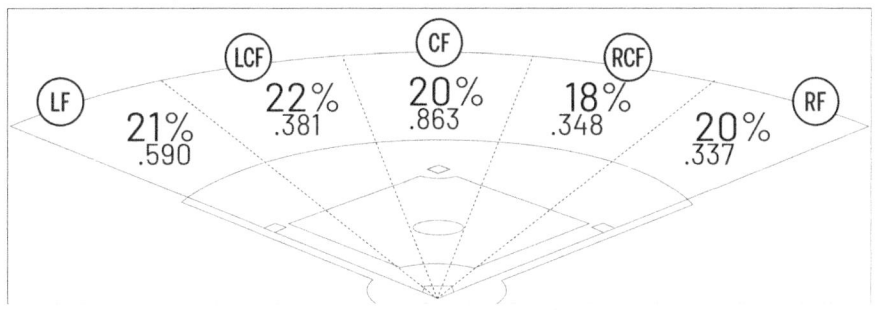

Strike Zone vs LHP   **Strike Zone vs RHP**

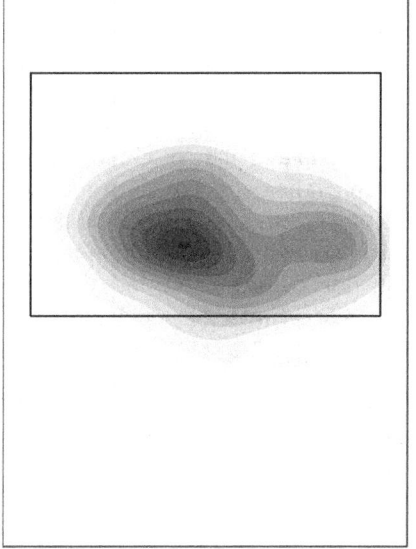

Nick Williams RF

Born: 09/08/93   Age: 25   Bats: L   Throws: L
Height: 6'3"   Weight: 195   Origin: Round 2, 2012 Draft (#93 overall)

YEAR	TEAM	LVL	AGE	PA	R	2B	3B	HR	RBI	BB	K	SB	CS	AVG/OBP/SLG
2016	LEH	AAA	22	527	78	33	6	13	64	19	136	6	4	.258/.287/.427
2017	LEH	AAA	23	306	43	16	2	15	44	16	90	5	4	.280/.328/.511
2017	PHI	MLB	23	343	45	14	4	12	55	20	97	1	2	.288/.338/.473
2018	PHI	MLB	24	448	53	12	3	17	50	32	111	3	2	.256/.324/.425
2019	PHI	MLB	25	194	21	9	1	7	24	10	55	1	1	.239/.289/.417

Breakout: 13%   Improve: 46%   Collapse: 18%   Attrition: 18%   MLB: 94%
Comparables: Oswaldo Arcia, Travis Snider, Wladimir Balentien

How do you properly describe a single season in which one player experiences both the "Eureka!" moment of things beginning to click and, later, the forlorn walking back of that same revelation? Whatever phrase you deem best, it's likely some form of the word "uncertain" will be lurking nearby. So it goes for Williams, who looked to be experiencing a breakthrough with regular starts from late May through the end of August: His .270/.339/.457 line in 307 plate appearances is awfully close to the slash Williams put up in his stellar rookie season. Then September hit, shoulder and finger injuries surfaced, and Williams barely (but successfully) played enough to tank his batting line. In spite of all that, it feels reasonable to take heart in Williams's overall improvements in pitch recognition and plate discipline. He remains a bit messy in right field, and his arm might be better suited to left field than right, but adjusting Williams's position is rather low on the Phillies' list of priorities right now. He's a mid-division regular who'll command more respect at the plate if his disciplinary adjustments are for real, with the potential to surprise those who may have missed or dismissed his midsummer hot streak.

YEAR	TEAM	LVL	AGE	PA	DRC+	VORP	BABIP	BRR	FRAA	WARP
2016	LEH	AAA	22	527	90	10.7	.325	-0.7	LF(50): 1.9, CF(38): 2.0	0.4
2017	LEH	AAA	23	306	119	14.6	.358	0.4	RF(37): 6.2, LF(17): 1.5	1.5
2017	PHI	MLB	23	343	93	19.3	.375	-0.8	RF(58): -5.9, CF(16): -2.0	-0.3
2018	PHI	MLB	24	448	98	11.0	.312	-1.4	RF(95): -9.8, LF(19): -1.5	-0.4
2019	PHI	MLB	25	194	85	2.3	.306	-0.2	LF -1, RF 0	0.1

Nick Williams, continued

Batted Ball Distribution

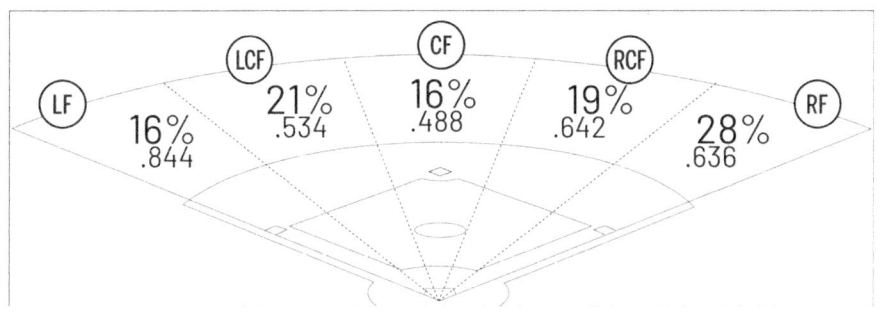

Strike Zone vs LHP

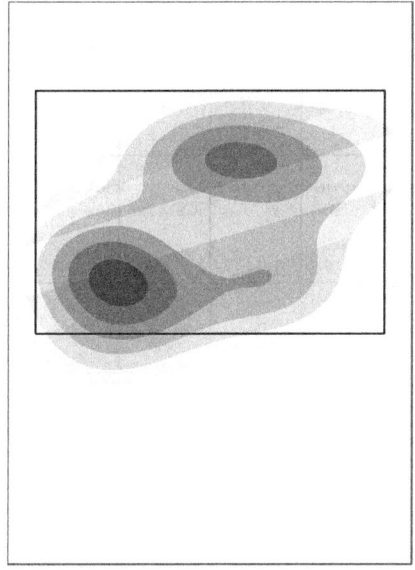

Strike Zone vs RHP

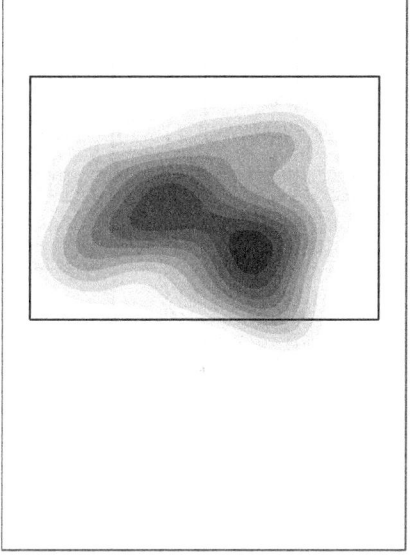

Jose Alvarez LHP

Born: 05/06/89 Age: 30 Bats: L Throws: L
Height: 5'11" Weight: 180 Origin: International Free Agent, 2005

YEAR	TEAM	LVL	AGE	W	L	SV	G	GS	IP	H	HR	BB/9	K/9	K	GB%	BABIP
2016	SLC	AAA	27	1	0	0	5	0	7^1	5	0	6.1	8.6	7	50%	.278
2016	ANA	MLB	27	1	3	0	64	0	57^1	71	4	2.4	8.0	51	46%	.362
2017	SLC	AAA	28	0	0	0	9	0	11^2	10	0	1.5	7.7	10	44%	.294
2017	ANA	MLB	28	0	3	1	64	0	48^2	50	7	2.2	8.3	45	39%	.309
2018	ANA	MLB	29	6	4	1	76	0	63	51	3	3.1	8.4	59	48%	.274
2019	PHI	MLB	30	2	2	0	36	0	38	37	5	3.6	8.8	38	44%	.296

Breakout: 29% Improve: 54% Collapse: 24% Attrition: 13% MLB: 93%
Comparables: Burke Badenhop, Jeremy Jeffress, Brandon League

Alvarez is a low-ceiling, high-floor middle-inning option. There is nothing incredible to say about him other than he does his job decently. He is so dull, his clubhouse nickname is Jose Alvarez. His favorite spice is oxygen. His fastball tops out at 92 mph. He wrote his dissertation on the practical applications of linoleum. He's a left-handed reliever and has been perfectly dependable for four years, and will continue to be dependable for a couple more. Middle relievers are like umpires; the ones you recognize are usually the ones with major flaws. When the bases are loaded and the manager needs some sanity in the game, sometimes you want a pitcher out there with a proclivity for watching paint dry.

YEAR	TEAM	LVL	AGE	WHIP	ERA	DRA	WARP	MPH	FB%	WHF	CSP
2016	SLC	AAA	27	1.36	2.45	2.93	0.2				
2016	ANA	MLB	27	1.50	3.45	4.87	0.1	92.9	45.8	11.6	47.1
2017	SLC	AAA	28	1.03	2.31	4.27	0.1				
2017	ANA	MLB	28	1.27	3.88	4.35	0.4	92.8	55.9	12	45.6
2018	ANA	MLB	29	1.16	2.71	3.82	0.8	93.3	57	11.5	47.9
2019	PHI	MLB	30	1.35	4.33	4.49	0.1	92.3	53.7	11.6	46.8

Jose Alvarez, continued

Pitch Shape vs LHH

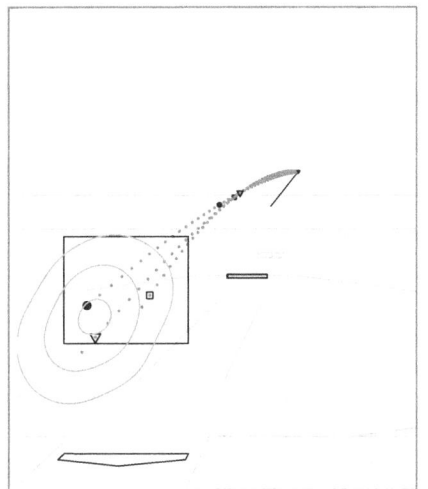

Pitch Shape vs RHH

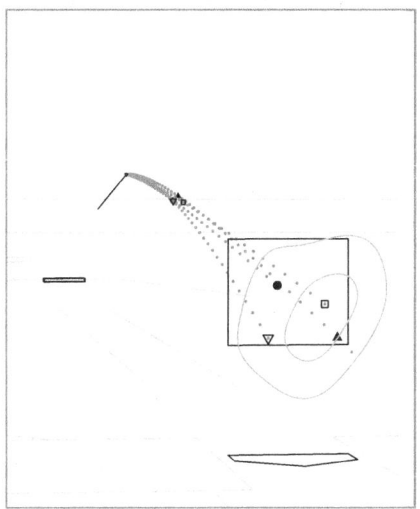

Type		Frequency	Velocity	H Movement	V Movement
●	Fastball	37.3%	92.3 [99]	7.5 [96]	-14.3 [105]
□	Sinker	19.7%	91.9 [97]	14.8 [82]	-19.4 [103]
+	Cutter	2.3%	87.5 [92]	-2.4 [103]	-23.9 [99]
▲	Changeup	14.4%	81.9 [86]	13.2 [90]	-30.8 [90]
×	Splitter				
▽	Slider	26.3%	83.2 [94]	-4.1 [97]	-33.2 [99]
◇	Curveball				
⊕	Slow Curveball				
✳	Knuckleball				
▼	Screwball				

Phillies Player Analysis - 51

Victor Arano   RHP

Born: 02/07/95   Age: 24   Bats: R   Throws: R
Height: 6'2"   Weight: 200   Origin: International Free Agent, 2013

YEAR	TEAM	LVL	AGE	W	L	SV	G	GS	IP	H	HR	BB/9	K/9	K	GB%	BABIP
2016	CLR	A+	21	4	1	4	35	0	63	52	4	2.1	10.1	71	38%	.296
2016	REA	AA	21	1	1	1	11	0	16^2	11	2	2.2	13.0	24	47%	.250
2017	REA	AA	22	1	2	9	32	0	38^2	39	7	2.6	8.8	38	40%	.296
2017	PHI	MLB	22	1	0	0	10	0	10^2	6	0	3.4	11.0	13	44%	.240
2018	PHI	MLB	23	1	2	3	60	0	59^1	54	6	2.6	9.1	60	40%	.296
2019	PHI	MLB	24	2	2	0	36	0	38	35	6	3.5	10.0	43	40%	.295

Breakout: 30%   Improve: 47%   Collapse: 9%   Attrition: 19%   MLB: 69%
Comparables: Manny Corpas, Brandon Beachy, Chris Ray

It's not a stretch to consider Arano the best reliever in the entire Phillies organization. The 24-year-old may not have the best pure stuff—that title belongs to Seranthony Dominguez—but Arano's total package of lively four-seam and two-seam fastballs with a disappearing slider have made him awfully tough to square up thus far. He wasn't quite as dominant over a full season as he was in his short time up in 2017, but he was still awfully effective. He'll even show some multi-inning flexibility when needed, which feels more and more like a critical characteristic of a bullpen piece in this age. The Phillies aren't light on vibrant relief arms, but not only is Arano already arguably the best among them, better things might still be in store.

YEAR	TEAM	LVL	AGE	WHIP	ERA	DRA	WARP	MPH	FB%	WHF	CSP
2016	CLR	A+	21	1.06	2.29	2.87	1.6				
2016	REA	AA	21	0.90	2.16	1.43	0.7				
2017	REA	AA	22	1.29	4.19	3.39	0.6				
2017	PHI	MLB	22	0.94	1.69	2.82	0.3	95.5	44.2	20.4	46.1
2018	PHI	MLB	23	1.20	2.73	3.56	0.9	95.8	40.2	16.9	45.7
2019	PHI	MLB	24	1.29	4.28	4.46	0.2	95.6	41.9	17.9	47.3

Victor Arano, continued

Pitch Shape vs LHH

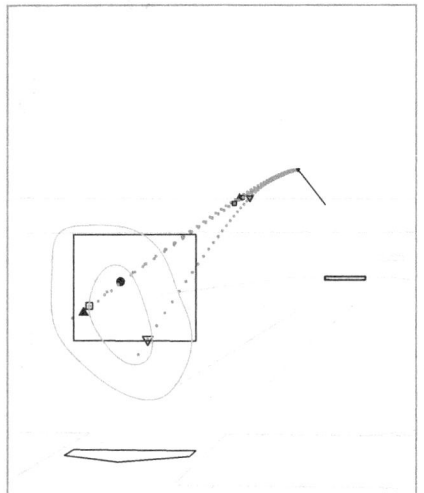

Pitch Shape vs RHH

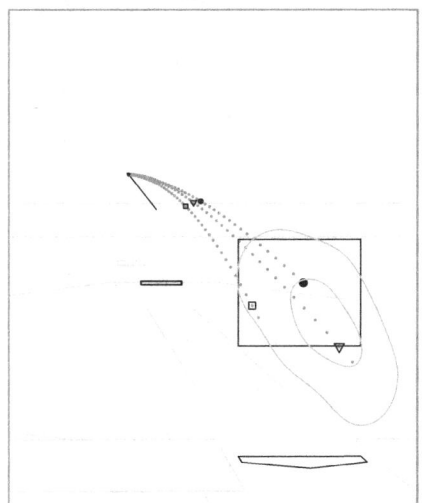

Type	Frequency	Velocity	H Movement	V Movement
● Fastball	26.2%	94.4 [106]	-9.8 [85]	-13.5 [107]
☐ Sinker	14.0%	93.6 [106]	-13.8 [90]	-17.9 [108]
+ Cutter				
▲ Changeup	3.7%	88.1 [111]	-12.1 [96]	-21.2 [118]
✕ Splitter				
▽ Slider	56.1%	85 [102]	1.3 [85]	-29.2 [111]
◇ Curveball				
⊕ Slow Curveball				
✴ Knuckleball				
▼ Screwball				

Jake Arrieta RHP
Born: 03/06/86   Age: 33   Bats: R   Throws: R
Height: 6'4"   Weight: 225   Origin: Round 5, 2007 Draft (#159 overall)

YEAR	TEAM	LVL	AGE	W	L	SV	G	GS	IP	H	HR	BB/9	K/9	K	GB%	BABIP
2016	CHN	MLB	30	18	8	0	31	31	197^1	138	16	3.5	8.7	190	54%	.241
2017	CHN	MLB	31	14	10	0	30	30	168^1	150	23	2.9	8.7	163	46%	.279
2018	PHI	MLB	32	10	11	0	31	31	172^2	165	21	3.0	7.2	138	52%	.289
2019	PHI	MLB	33	11	9	0	30	30	171	148	20	3.0	8.4	159	49%	.276

Breakout: 14%   Improve: 45%   Collapse: 17%   Attrition: 11%   MLB: 96%
Comparables: Zack Greinke, Clay Buchholz, Tim Hudson

Compared to 2017, Arrieta had a higher ERA, lower K%, higher BB%, fewer swinging strikes, fewer quality starts, and permitted more and harder contact across 4.1 more innings...but saw increases over his 2017 WARP and rWAR. It's hard to discern which is more true: That Arrieta is in the midst of a continuing decline, or that he's still above-average in the eyes of a league whose attitudes toward starting pitchers continues to shift rapidly around him. (Or that going from the Cubs' defense to the Phillies interpretation is an act of courage worthy of a medal.) Make no mistake: His drops in power metrics like strikeouts and whiffs were even sharper this year than last, and the Snake of 2015-16 isn't walking through that door. But his velocity recovered, and his health held up through 30-plus starts for a fourth consecutive year, and there's something to be said for both of those accomplishments in the face of pointed offseason skepticism even as he appeared to lose steam over his final four starts in September. However much he has left in the tank, he'll need better backup from his defense if he's to stand any chance of successfully completing this late-stage metamorphosis into a pitch-to-contact style.

YEAR	TEAM	LVL	AGE	WHIP	ERA	DRA	WARP	MPH	FB%	WHF	CSP
2016	CHN	MLB	30	1.08	3.10	2.76	5.9	96.3	65.7	11.4	46.2
2017	CHN	MLB	31	1.22	3.53	4.09	2.8	93.8	64.3	9.3	49.1
2018	PHI	MLB	32	1.29	3.96	4.08	2.4	94.8	55.8	8.8	50.1
2019	PHI	MLB	33	1.17	4.03	4.23	1.6	93.9	60.5	9.6	48.2

Jake Arrieta, continued

Pitch Shape vs LHH

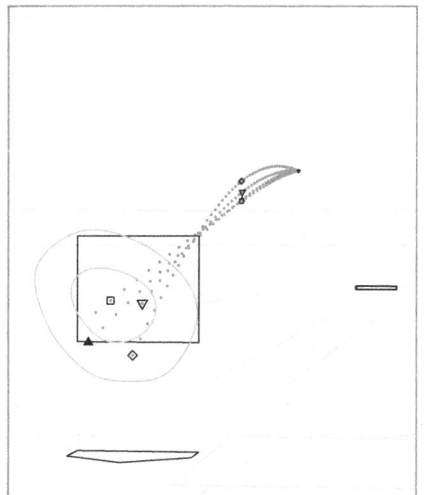

Pitch Shape vs RHH

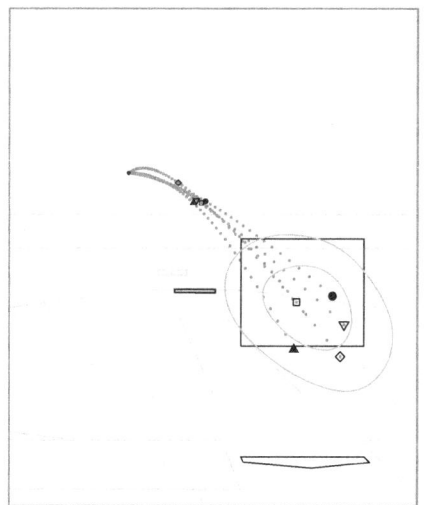

Type		Frequency	Velocity	H Movement	V Movement
●	Fastball	2.0%	92.9 [101]	-6.5 [101]	-15.6 [100]
□	Sinker	53.8%	93.6 [105]	-13.2 [95]	-19.5 [103]
+	Cutter				
▲	Changeup	10.4%	88.5 [113]	-12.5 [93]	-29.2 [94]
×	Splitter				
▽	Slider	23.6%	89.8 [124]	5 [101]	-25.1 [124]
◇	Curveball	10.3%	81.2 [110]	12.1 [118]	-47.9 [100]
✦	Slow Curveball				
✱	Knuckleball				
▼	Screwball				

Austin Davis LHP

Born: 02/03/93 Age: 26 Bats: L Throws: L
Height: 6'4" Weight: 245 Origin: Round 12, 2014 Draft (#352 overall)

YEAR	TEAM	LVL	AGE	W	L	SV	G	GS	IP	H	HR	BB/9	K/9	K	GB%	BABIP
2016	LWD	A	23	1	0	1	7	0	13	6	0	1.4	11.8	17	45%	.207
2016	CLR	A+	23	0	1	1	11	1	15^1	16	0	2.3	10.6	18	40%	.356
2017	CLR	A+	24	2	0	1	10	0	22^1	19	1	1.2	11.7	29	39%	.327
2017	REA	AA	24	4	2	1	32	0	47	45	3	3.8	8.8	46	44%	.328
2018	REA	AA	25	1	1	0	4	0	7	7	1	2.6	12.9	10	68%	.333
2018	LEH	AAA	25	0	1	0	24	0	31^1	23	2	2.3	11.5	40	37%	.284
2018	PHI	MLB	25	1	2	0	32	0	34^2	35	4	3.1	9.9	38	42%	.326
2019	PHI	MLB	26	1	1	0	26	0	27	25	4	4.0	10.1	31	41%	.296

Breakout: 17% Improve: 24% Collapse: 8% Attrition: 18% MLB: 44%
Comparables: Lucas Luetge, Mayckol Guaipe, Royce Ring

You don't have to look too closely at Davis's game logs to see where it all began to crumble for the 25-year-old rookie. On July 24, Davis pitched in his third straight game and threw 35 pitches, holding down the 14th and 15th innings of a game that eventually went 16. It was the first time Davis had worked three straight as a pro, and the remainder of his season—directly or indirectly—bore the effects of that effort. Davis would eventually miss two weeks in August with a lower back issue, the same ailment that felled him in 2016, and opponents teed off on him (.940 OPS) even when he was healthy. When everything's going right, Davis will sit 94 with a slider and good separation on his tumbling changeup, and he carries a minor league usage pedigree geared toward higher pitch counts and multiple innings of work. The 2014 12th-rounder has some durability concerns to shake, but otherwise shows all the makings of a reliable bullpen piece after the winter allows for a hard reset.

YEAR	TEAM	LVL	AGE	WHIP	ERA	DRA	WARP	MPH	FB%	WHF	CSP
2016	LWD	A	23	0.62	0.00	2.20	0.4				
2016	CLR	A+	23	1.30	5.28	2.07	0.5				
2017	CLR	A+	24	0.99	2.01	2.12	0.7				
2017	REA	AA	24	1.38	2.87	4.07	0.4				
2018	REA	AA	25	1.29	3.86	2.72	0.2				
2018	LEH	AAA	25	0.99	2.59	3.17	0.7				
2018	PHI	MLB	25	1.36	4.15	4.29	0.3	95.5	47.9	12.4	47.6
2019	PHI	MLB	26	1.35	4.40	4.55	0.1	95.1	48.7	12.6	48.4

Austin Davis, continued

Pitch Shape vs LHH

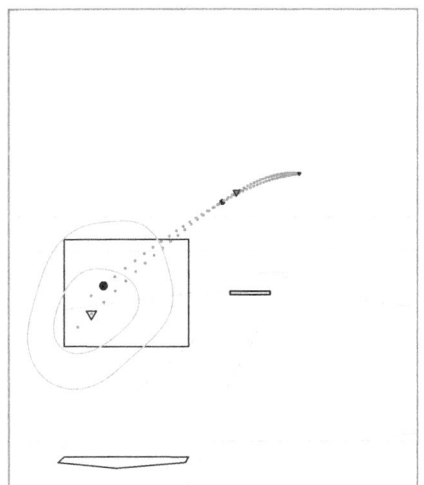

Pitch Shape vs RHH

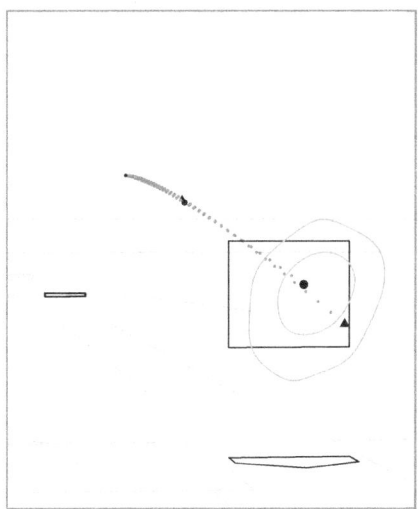

Type	Frequency	Velocity	H Movement	V Movement
● Fastball	47.6%	93.6 [104]	7.2 [97]	-14 [106]
☐ Sinker	0.3%	92.4 [100]	15.7 [74]	-18.3 [107]
+ Cutter				
▲ Changeup	23.8%	84 [95]	12.2 [95]	-24.6 [108]
✕ Splitter				
▽ Slider	28.3%	84.8 [101]	-2.3 [89]	-28.9 [112]
◇ Curveball				
⊕ Slow Curveball				
✳ Knuckleball				
▼ Screwball				

Philadelphia Phillies 2019

Enyel De Los Santos RHP
Born: 12/25/95 Age: 23 Bats: R Throws: R
Height: 6'3" Weight: 170 Origin: International Free Agent, 2014

YEAR	TEAM	LVL	AGE	W	L	SV	G	GS	IP	H	HR	BB/9	K/9	K	GB%	BABIP
2016	FTW	A	20	3	2	0	11	7	52^2	38	2	2.4	7.7	45	41%	.242
2016	LEL	A+	20	5	3	0	15	15	68^1	70	11	3.2	6.8	52	38%	.291
2017	SAN	AA	21	10	6	0	26	24	150	131	12	2.9	8.3	138	45%	.290
2018	LEH	AAA	22	10	5	0	22	22	126^2	104	12	3.1	7.8	110	42%	.264
2018	PHI	MLB	22	1	0	0	7	2	19	19	2	3.8	7.1	15	51%	.309
2019	PHI	MLB	23	3	2	0	8	8	40	37	6	3.2	8.6	38	40%	.291

Breakout: 13% Improve: 21% Collapse: 16% Attrition: 34% MLB: 54%
Comparables: Tyler Mahle, Eddie Butler, Jake Thompson

What they've long lacked in stars, the Phillies have compensated for in acquiring useful players in trades for their rentals. Count EDLS among those. The 23-year-old—acquired before the 2018 season for Freddy Galvis—pumps 95 with a solid changeup as a starter, but lacks a quality third pitch. That, coupled with the Phillies' relatively strong starting pitching depth in the upper minors, may make De Los Santos an appealing candidate for the Seranthony Dominguez Treatment. It's too early to assume or even to try to quantify his already live arm in short stints, but with Nola, Arrieta, and Pivetta firmly holding three rotation spots while other organizational favorites like Cole Irvin, Ranger Suarez and JoJo Romero are nearly ready to compete with Vince Velasquez and Zach Eflin, De Los Santos's best option for holding down a Major League job might just be in the bullpen. It helps to think he just might flourish in that role.

YEAR	TEAM	LVL	AGE	WHIP	ERA	DRA	WARP	MPH	FB%	WHF	CSP
2016	FTW	A	20	0.99	2.91	3.50	0.9				
2016	LEL	A+	20	1.38	4.35	4.19	1.0				
2017	SAN	AA	21	1.19	3.78	3.25	3.4				
2018	LEH	AAA	22	1.16	2.63	3.78	2.5				
2018	PHI	MLB	22	1.42	4.74	4.97	0.0	97.1	60.3	10.8	50.2
2019	PHI	MLB	23	1.27	4.47	4.71	0.2	97.0	62.5	11.1	52

Enyel De Los Santos, continued

Pitch Shape vs LHH

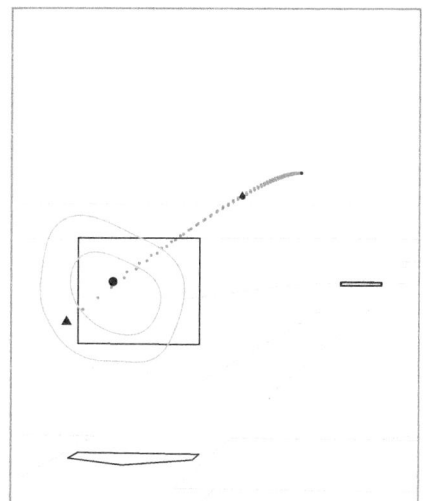

Pitch Shape vs RHH

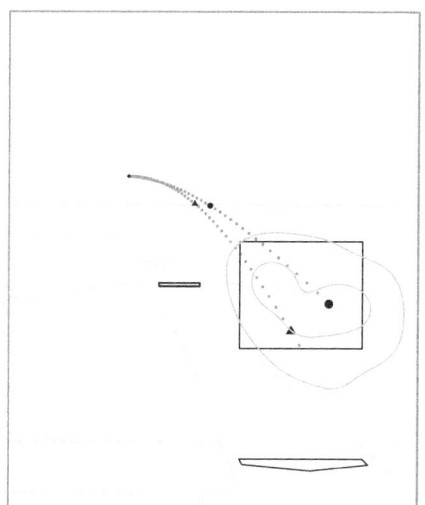

Type	Frequency	Velocity	H Movement	V Movement
● Fastball	60.3%	94.9 [108]	-9.9 [85]	-17.2 [95]
☐ Sinker				
+ Cutter				
▲ Changeup	25.1%	86.9 [106]	-14.3 [84]	-26.6 [102]
✕ Splitter				
▽ Slider	5.1%	82.3 [90]	4.8 [100]	-36.8 [89]
◇ Curveball	9.6%	77.2 [95]	4.2 [85]	-45.2 [106]
⊕ Slow Curveball				
✳ Knuckleball				
▼ Screwball				

Phillies Player Analysis - 59

Seranthony Dominguez   RHP
Born: 11/25/94   Age: 24   Bats: R   Throws: R
Height: 6'1"   Weight: 185   Origin: International Free Agent, 2011

YEAR	TEAM	LVL	AGE	W	L	SV	G	GS	IP	H	HR	BB/9	K/9	K	GB%	BABIP
2016	WPT	A-	21	1	1	0	3	3	17	8	0	2.1	7.9	15	57%	.170
2016	LWD	A	21	5	2	0	10	10	48¹	34	2	3.7	9.3	50	58%	.271
2017	CLR	A+	22	4	4	0	15	13	62¹	51	6	4.3	10.8	75	45%	.306
2018	REA	AA	23	1	2	0	8	0	13	8	0	1.4	12.5	18	52%	.296
2018	PHI	MLB	23	2	5	16	53	0	58	32	4	3.4	11.5	74	56%	.220
2019	PHI	MLB	24	3	2	16	52	0	54	43	5	4.2	11.0	67	48%	.285

Breakout: 25%   Improve: 55%   Collapse: 12%   Attrition: 13%   MLB: 91%
Comparables: Rubby De La Rosa, Matt Moore, Edwin Diaz

There's something beautifully chaotic about watching Seranthony Dominguez pitch. What starts as a simple, compact wind-up gradually transforms and unfurls into a pinwheeling trebuchet of a delivery, an explosion of arm action that allows him to throw 99 MPH cutters and wipeout sliders. The changeup is still a bit of a work in progress—a reason he was converted from a starter to a reliever before the 2018 season began—but the established two-pitch mix is more than good enough to build on. That being said, whoever's doing the catching while Seranthony is on the mound will need to be sure they've limbered up while trying to corral the pitches that are simply too nasty to travel the full 60.5 feet; any time more than 1 percent of your pitches go down as wild pitches, well, that's a lot of runner movement that could be prevented. Really, though, in the context of his first professional season as a full-time reliever, it's hard to see 2018 as anything but a successful effort for Dominguez, and goes a long way toward stabilizing the club's 2019 relief outlook.

YEAR	TEAM	LVL	AGE	WHIP	ERA	DRA	WARP	MPH	FB%	WHF	CSP
2016	WPT	A-	21	0.71	2.12	3.14	0.4				
2016	LWD	A	21	1.12	2.42	3.74	0.8				
2017	CLR	A+	22	1.30	3.61	3.28	1.4				
2018	REA	AA	23	0.77	2.08	3.09	0.3				
2018	PHI	MLB	23	0.93	2.95	3.00	1.3	99.5	66.6	16.3	49.1
2019	PHI	MLB	24	1.23	3.47	3.79	0.6	99.3	68.6	16.8	50.6

Seranthony Dominguez, continued

Pitch Shape vs LHH

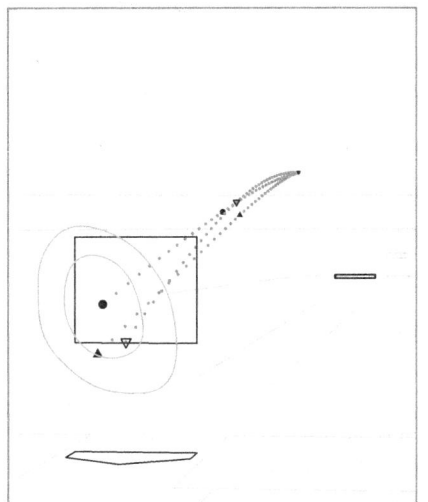

Pitch Shape vs RHH

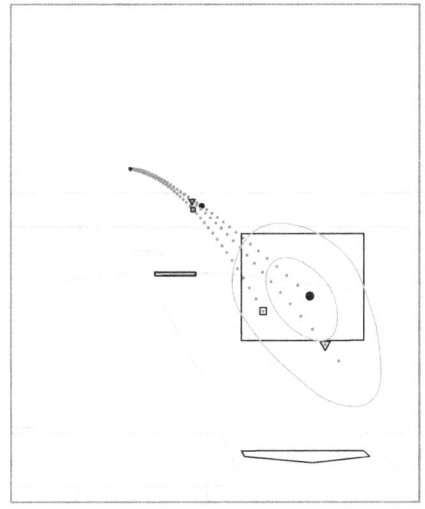

Type	Frequency	Velocity	H Movement	V Movement
● Fastball	60.3%	98.4 [119]	-0.6 [128]	-14.1 [105]
☐ Sinker	6.3%	98.6 [130]	-11.7 [108]	-17.2 [110]
+ Cutter				
▲ Changeup	6.4%	91.6 [125]	-13.3 [89]	-23.6 [111]
✕ Splitter				
▽ Slider	27.0%	89.2 [121]	5.2 [102]	-30.2 [108]
◇ Curveball				
⊕ Slow Curveball				
✳ Knuckleball				
▼ Screwball				

Zach Eflin RHP

Born: 04/08/94   Age: 25   Bats: R   Throws: R
Height: 6'6"   Weight: 215   Origin: Round 1, 2012 Draft (#33 overall)

YEAR	TEAM	LVL	AGE	W	L	SV	G	GS	IP	H	HR	BB/9	K/9	K	GB%	BABIP
2016	LEH	AAA	22	5	2	0	11	11	68¹	49	2	1.4	7.2	55	47%	.245
2016	PHI	MLB	22	3	5	0	11	11	63¹	67	12	2.4	4.4	31	37%	.261
2017	LEH	AAA	23	1	4	0	8	7	43¹	48	3	3.1	7.9	38	41%	.346
2017	PHI	MLB	23	1	5	0	11	11	64¹	79	16	1.7	4.9	35	46%	.297
2018	LEH	AAA	24	2	2	0	4	4	20	20	0	2.2	6.8	15	46%	.317
2018	PHI	MLB	24	11	8	0	24	24	128	130	16	2.6	8.6	123	43%	.309
2019	PHI	MLB	25	8	7	0	24	24	127	118	17	2.6	8.8	124	42%	.290

Breakout: 15%   Improve: 45%   Collapse: 25%   Attrition: 33%   MLB: 85%
Comparables: Matt Wisler, Brett Oberholtzer, Vance Worley

When you're 6'6", it's pretty important to have healthy knees. They do a lot of work supporting that much human body! And when you're a 6'6" pitcher who needs strong knees to hold up to hours of standing and driving and planting, the demand is even greater. Given the trouble Eflin's knees gave him for years—finally addressed with surgery on both in late 2016—it's both understandable and convenient that a lot the struggles in his first two seasons could at least partially be blamed on them. Eflin started well, stringing together five consecutive wonderful starts in June against tough competition: The Cubs, Milwaukee twice, the Nationals, and the Yankees. He started leaking oil in mid-August, though, and had to putter his way through September before eventually admitting his side had been bothering him. Thus ended another intriguing but confusing season. Can Eflin's body hold up for 30 starts? Can he do what he did this past June for more than one month at a time? Will he be squeezed out in favor of the next batch of starters? As it stands right now, Eflin packs plenty of enticement into his stuff and should find Major League work for a few years if his body doesn't continue to betray him. It's just a shame his body didn't come with a warranty.

YEAR	TEAM	LVL	AGE	WHIP	ERA	DRA	WARP	MPH	FB%	WHF	CSP
2016	LEH	AAA	22	0.88	2.90	4.01	1.0				
2016	PHI	MLB	22	1.33	5.54	6.62	-0.9	96.0	63.5	6.7	51.1
2017	LEH	AAA	23	1.45	4.57	4.38	0.6				
2017	PHI	MLB	23	1.41	6.16	5.62	0.0	95.5	68.1	7.6	51
2018	LEH	AAA	24	1.25	4.05	3.69	0.4				
2018	PHI	MLB	24	1.30	4.36	4.67	1.0	96.4	58.2	11.5	51.4
2019	PHI	MLB	25	1.21	4.08	4.30	1.1	95.8	62.9	10	52.4

Zach Eflin, continued

Pitch Shape vs LHH

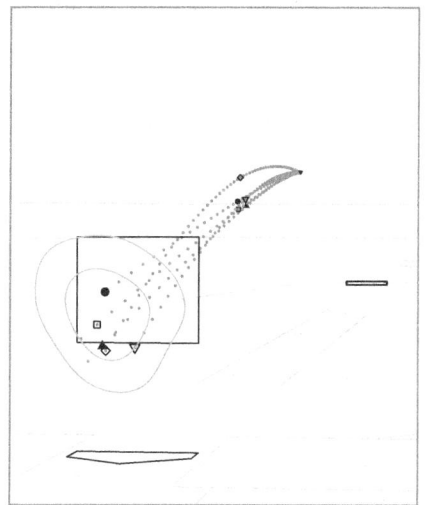

Pitch Shape vs RHH

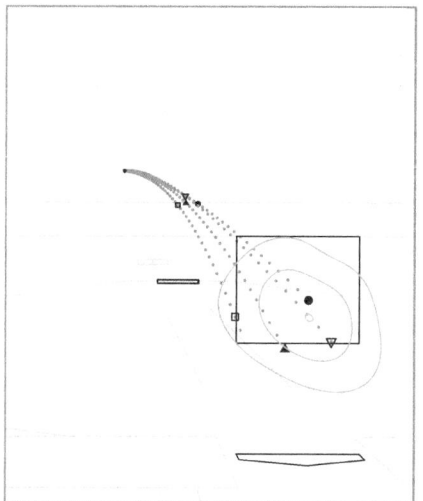

Type	Frequency	Velocity	H Movement	V Movement
● Fastball	46.5%	95.2 [108]	-7.7 [95]	-14.4 [104]
□ Sinker	11.8%	93.6 [105]	-14.3 [86]	-21.1 [97]
+ Cutter	2.5%	88.9 [101]	2.6 [104]	-24.4 [97]
▲ Changeup	11.1%	87.1 [107]	-12.2 [95]	-26.1 [104]
× Splitter				
▽ Slider	22.7%	86.1 [107]	4.6 [99]	-30.6 [107]
◇ Curveball	5.4%	77.9 [98]	10.3 [111]	-48.4 [99]
⊕ Slow Curveball				
✱ Knuckleball				
▼ Screwball				

Philadelphia Phillies 2019

Tommy Hunter   RHP
Born: 07/03/86   Age: 32   Bats: R   Throws: R
Height: 6'3"   Weight: 250   Origin: Round 1, 2007 Draft (#54 overall)

YEAR	TEAM	LVL	AGE	W	L	SV	G	GS	IP	H	HR	BB/9	K/9	K	GB%	BABIP
2016	CLE	MLB	29	2	2	0	21	0	21^2	21	1	2.1	7.1	17	53%	.308
2016	COH	AAA	29	2	1	1	14	2	15	14	2	1.2	6.0	10	46%	.261
2016	BAL	MLB	29	0	0	0	12	0	12^1	14	0	2.2	4.4	6	45%	.350
2017	TBA	MLB	30	3	5	1	61	0	58^2	43	6	2.1	9.8	64	46%	.259
2018	PHI	MLB	31	5	4	4	65	0	64	65	6	2.1	7.2	51	51%	.303
2019	PHI	MLB	32	2	2	2	47	0	49	48	7	3.1	8.1	44	47%	.295

Breakout: 19%   Improve: 38%   Collapse: 32%   Attrition: 13%   MLB: 93%
Comparables: Matt Wise, Anthony Swarzak, Luke Gregerson

Almost immediately, Hunter became the focal point of Philly fans' angst. He tweaked his hamstring at the end of Spring Training and missed the first three weeks of April, pitching through May as if starting from scratch. Though he could never erase the early numbers, from June through September, things calmed down considerably. While he was by no means spectacular, Hunter did hold opponents to a .297 OBP in the season's final four months, and did a fine job keeping the ball in the park. None of his last nine inherited runners scored, either. It's hard to explain *why* it continued to feel like every appearance Hunter made—even in the good months—felt like it teetered on the brink of disaster, but we'd be willing to excuse that on account of the Negadelphia-colored glasses. It does, however, appear that Hunter's huge K% spike in Tampa Bay in 2017 was more fluke than foreshadowing, and anyone who pitches to more contact in this day and age walks a fine tightrope.

YEAR	TEAM	LVL	AGE	WHIP	ERA	DRA	WARP	MPH	FB%	WHF	CSP
2016	CLE	MLB	29	1.20	3.74	5.09	0.0	96.7	84.4	10	51.2
2016	COH	AAA	29	1.07	3.00	3.48	0.3				
2016	BAL	MLB	29	1.38	2.19	4.98	0.0	96.9	84.4	11.9	51.1
2017	TBA	MLB	30	0.97	2.61	2.99	1.4	97.6	74.2	12.9	46.6
2018	PHI	MLB	31	1.25	3.80	4.54	0.3	97.2	86.2	11.5	49.1
2019	PHI	MLB	32	1.33	4.51	4.62	0.1	96.3	80.9	11.8	48.4

Tommy Hunter, continued

Pitch Shape vs LHH
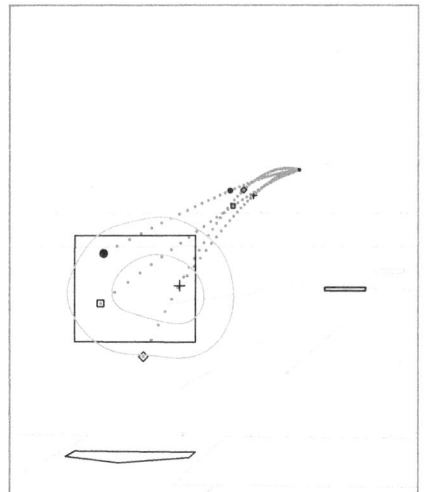

Pitch Shape vs RHH
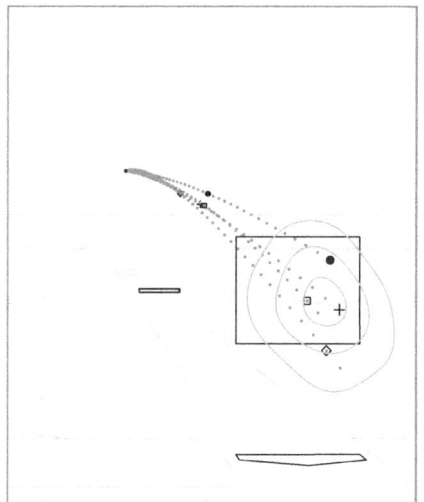

Type	Frequency	Velocity	H Movement	V Movement
● Fastball	8.3%	96.8 [114]	-6 [103]	-11.6 [113]
□ Sinker	33.5%	96.2 [119]	-11.4 [110]	-16.1 [114]
+ Cutter	44.4%	93.9 [130]	2.5 [104]	-18.1 [123]
▲ Changeup				
× Splitter				
▽ Slider	0.1%	84.7 [101]	12.2 [132]	-37 [88]
◇ Curveball	13.7%	84.9 [124]	9.4 [106]	-38.7 [121]
⊕ Slow Curveball				
✳ Knuckleball				
▼ Screwball				

Phillies Player Analysis

Philadelphia Phillies 2019

Adam Morgan   LHP
Born: 02/27/90   Age: 29   Bats: L   Throws: L
Height: 6'1"   Weight: 200   Origin: Round 3, 2011 Draft (#120 overall)

YEAR	TEAM	LVL	AGE	W	L	SV	G	GS	IP	H	HR	BB/9	K/9	K	GB%	BABIP
2016	LEH	AAA	26	6	1	0	8	7	50^1	43	4	1.8	9.3	52	42%	.293
2016	PHI	MLB	26	2	11	0	23	21	113^1	141	23	2.3	7.5	95	40%	.331
2017	LEH	AAA	27	0	1	0	12	0	17^1	19	1	2.6	7.3	14	44%	.340
2017	PHI	MLB	27	3	3	0	37	0	54^2	51	10	3.0	10.4	63	45%	.297
2018	PHI	MLB	28	0	2	1	67	0	49^1	49	5	4.0	9.1	50	54%	.324
2019	PHI	MLB	29	2	1	0	31	0	32	29	3	3.4	9.7	35	46%	.296

Breakout: 25%   Improve: 50%   Collapse: 14%   Attrition: 13%   MLB: 78%
Comparables: Boof Bonser, Glen Perkins, Brian Matusz

You thought you had us fooled, Morgan. You thought we'd all bit on your 2017 second half as The Real Deal, a Platonic Leftiness that would solidify your place in the Phillies' bullpen for multiple years. Instead, you pulled off your mask to reveal that you were actually J.C. Romero all along. Sure, sure, you kept opponents' slugging numbers down and allowed only one homer to a lefty all year, but your walk totals took off as your strikeout tallies slipped backward, and next thing we all knew LHBs had a .350 OBP against you. Maybe your late-season velocity slip was to blame; maybe it was the disproportionate amount of batted balls that dropped in for hits; maybe hitters just had a better feel for your approach in your second season of full-time relieving. Or maybe you just need that mask back.

YEAR	TEAM	LVL	AGE	WHIP	ERA	DRA	WARP	MPH	FB%	WHF	CSP
2016	LEH	AAA	26	1.05	3.04	2.19	1.8				
2016	PHI	MLB	26	1.50	6.04	4.83	0.7	93.6	49.3	11.6	43.6
2017	LEH	AAA	27	1.38	4.67	3.21	0.4				
2017	PHI	MLB	27	1.26	4.12	3.12	1.2	96.3	33.2	17.5	44.8
2018	PHI	MLB	28	1.44	3.83	4.31	0.4	95.7	34.9	13.1	48.5
2019	PHI	MLB	29	1.27	3.59	3.88	0.4	94.3	40.5	13.6	46

Adam Morgan, continued

Pitch Shape vs LHH

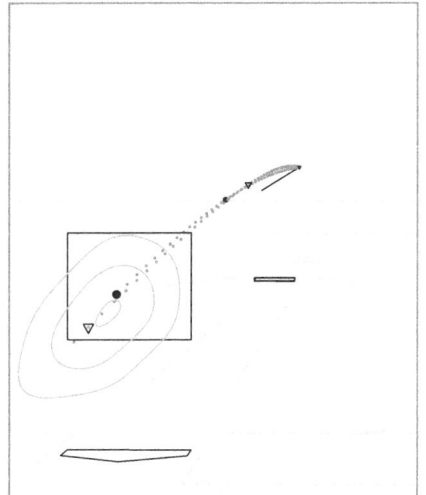

Pitch Shape vs RHH

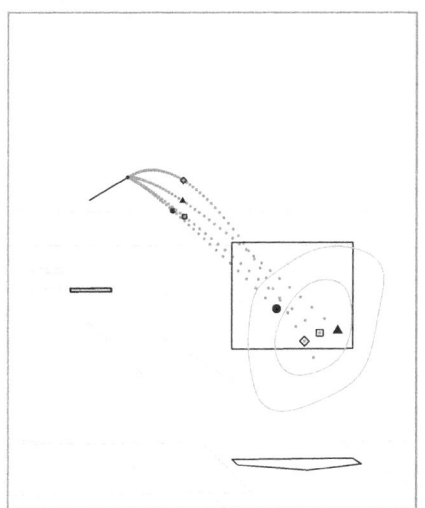

Type	Frequency	Velocity	H Movement	V Movement
● Fastball	21.9%	94.6 [107]	9.6 [86]	-14.7 [103]
☐ Sinker	13.1%	94.1 [108]	14.7 [83]	-18.8 [105]
+ Cutter				
▲ Changeup	15.3%	83.9 [94]	10.3 [105]	-25.8 [105]
× Splitter				
▽ Slider	42.0%	81.4 [86]	-13.3 [136]	-35.4 [93]
◇ Curveball	7.8%	78.5 [100]	-8.2 [102]	-50 [96]
⊕ Slow Curveball				
✳ Knuckleball				
▼ Screwball				

Hector Neris RHP
Born: 06/14/89 Age: 30 Bats: R Throws: R
Height: 6'2" Weight: 215 Origin: International Free Agent, 2010

YEAR	TEAM	LVL	AGE	W	L	SV	G	GS	IP	H	HR	BB/9	K/9	K	GB%	BABIP
2016	PHI	MLB	27	4	4	2	79	0	80^1	59	9	3.4	11.4	102	44%	.272
2017	PHI	MLB	28	4	5	26	74	0	74^2	68	9	3.1	10.4	86	35%	.306
2018	LEH	AAA	29	2	0	1	19	0	18^2	9	0	3.4	14.9	31	46%	.257
2018	PHI	MLB	29	1	3	11	53	0	47^2	46	11	3.0	14.3	76	33%	.354
2019	PHI	MLB	30	2	2	5	36	0	38	30	4	3.5	12.0	51	39%	.294

Breakout: 23%   Improve: 43%   Collapse: 25%   Attrition: 12%   MLB: 83%
Comparables: Pat Neshek, Vinnie Pestano, Danny Farquhar

Okay, what did we just watch? What happened out there? Who was that man wearing 50 in red pinstripes through June, and what did he do with the reliable dude who'd previously inhabited his body? Even better, who was the *other* man who emerged in August, striking everyone out like he was Craig Kimbrel? There are two clear-cut, distinct parts to Hector Neris's season pre- and post-option on June 29, and neither was much like the guy who pitched the previous three seasons. The first three months were agony, and the longer they drew on, the more it became reasonable to question whether Neris, somehow, had burned out. The Phillies have said a big part of Neris's disastrous first three months was due to hand placement at set, and pitch tipping, a nasty combo if you're a two-pitch guy. With a fix in place, Neris returned to strike out 35 of the final 69 batters, giving up just a .172 opp. AVG despite a .379 BABIP and zero home runs. He looked unstoppable, but more than that, he might just have saved his career.

YEAR	TEAM	LVL	AGE	WHIP	ERA	DRA	WARP	MPH	FB%	WHF	CSP
2016	PHI	MLB	27	1.11	2.58	3.15	1.7	96.9	45.3	16.7	45.7
2017	PHI	MLB	28	1.26	3.01	4.25	0.8	96.0	48.6	17.8	48.3
2018	LEH	AAA	29	0.86	1.45	2.34	0.6				
2018	PHI	MLB	29	1.30	5.10	2.36	1.4	96.6	47.1	20.5	46.5
2019	PHI	MLB	30	1.16	3.09	3.46	0.6	95.7	47	18.2	46.7

Hector Neris, continued

Pitch Shape vs LHH

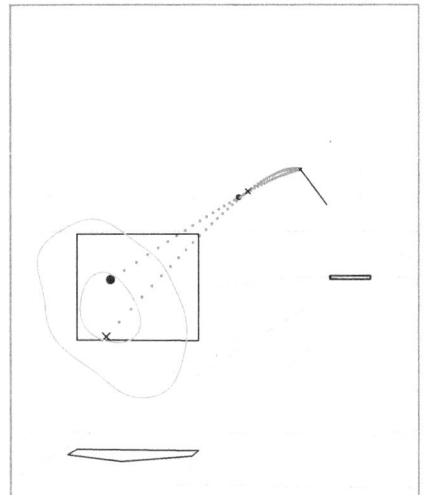

Pitch Shape vs RHH

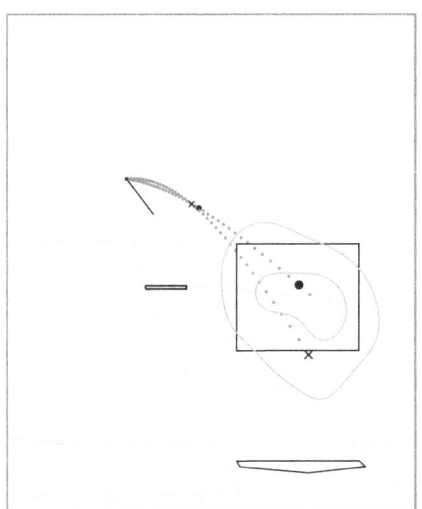

Type	Frequency	Velocity	H Movement	V Movement
● Fastball	42.2%	95.2 [109]	-7.2 [98]	-12.8 [109]
□ Sinker	4.9%	94.9 [112]	-14.3 [86]	-19.1 [104]
+ Cutter				
▲ Changeup				
✕ Splitter	49.2%	86.5 [104]	-9.5 [95]	-33 [85]
▽ Slider	3.6%	88.5 [118]	2.1 [88]	-25.7 [122]
◇ Curveball				
⊕ Slow Curveball				
✱ Knuckleball				
▼ Screwball				

Pat Neshek RHP

Born: 09/04/80 Age: 38 Bats: B Throws: R
Height: 6'3" Weight: 220 Origin: Round 6, 2002 Draft (#182 overall)

YEAR	TEAM	LVL	AGE	W	L	SV	G	GS	IP	H	HR	BB/9	K/9	K	GB%	BABIP
2016	HOU	MLB	35	2	2	0	60	0	47	33	6	2.1	8.2	43	37%	.216
2017	PHI	MLB	36	3	2	1	43	0	40^1	28	2	1.1	10.0	45	37%	.271
2017	COL	MLB	36	2	1	0	28	0	22	20	1	0.4	9.8	24	36%	.311
2018	PHI	MLB	37	3	2	5	30	0	24^1	23	2	1.8	5.5	15	41%	.266
2019	PHI	MLB	38	2	2	3	41	0	43	44	8	3.3	7.8	38	40%	.286

Breakout: 24% Improve: 38% Collapse: 30% Attrition: 8% MLB: 86%
Comparables: Rollie Fingers, Larry Andersen, Trevor Hoffman

You wouldn't be at fault if you thought Neshek could finish Darren Oliver-ing his way through his late thirties, suppressing opposing hitters in short bursts of exposure without being overpowering. At the very least, the 2017 season was a strong point of evidence in favor, as Neshek made 71 mostly excellent appearances between Philadelphia and Colorado. His K rate spiked (at age 37, no less), his walk rate took a tumble in parallel, and his home run rate even *decreased* after joining the Rockies. Neshek publicly expressed an affinity for pitching in Philadelphia, and so a reunion for 2018 made perfect sense. That was about the extent of the fairy tale, though: Neshek got hurt toward the end of Spring Training and missed the first three months of the year. Upon his return, he threw 11 consecutive scoreless appearances, but once that streak ended on August 3, the sidearmer limped through the end of the season. Whether that's a harbinger of a crash to come or merely a blip during what's been a remarkable stretch of pitching from the sideswiping righty is a question only because of his age.

YEAR	TEAM	LVL	AGE	WHIP	ERA	DRA	WARP	MPH	FB%	WHF	CSP
2016	HOU	MLB	35	0.94	3.06	3.56	0.8	92.0	38.9	11.9	54
2017	PHI	MLB	36	0.82	1.12	3.00	1.0	92.3	49.4	14.7	56.7
2017	COL	MLB	36	0.95	2.45	3.56	0.4	92.2	37.9	15	54.5
2018	PHI	MLB	37	1.15	2.59	4.73	0.1	90.9	39.5	11.3	56
2019	PHI	MLB	38	1.35	5.20	5.16	-0.2	90.4	41	12.8	54

Pat Neshek, continued

Pitch Shape vs LHH

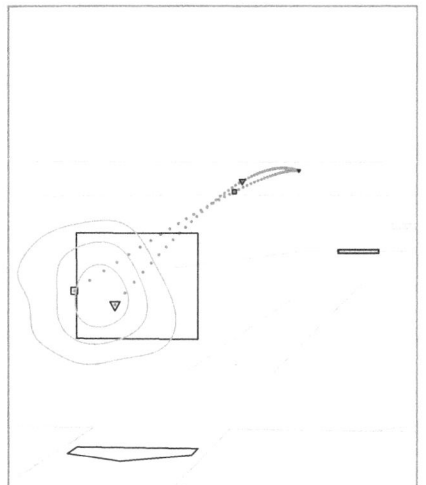

Pitch Shape vs RHH

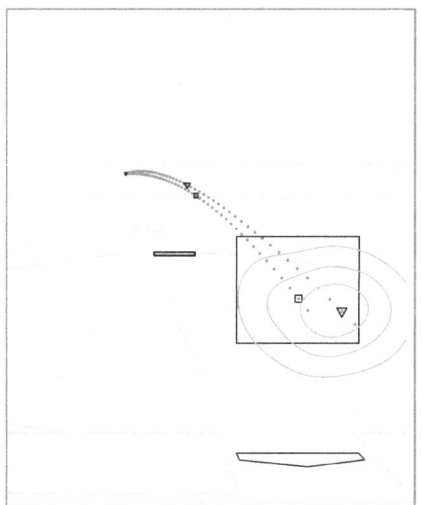

Type	Frequency	Velocity	H Movement	V Movement
● Fastball				
☐ Sinker	39.5%	89.4 [85]	-12.8 [99]	-22.5 [93]
+ Cutter				
▲ Changeup	0.8%	63.5 [13]	-5.5 [131]	-56 [15]
✕ Splitter				
▽ Slider	59.7%	81.5 [87]	3.8 [96]	-34.1 [97]
◇ Curveball				
⊕ Slow Curveball				
✳ Knuckleball				
▼ Screwball				

Philadelphia Phillies 2019

Juan Nicasio   RHP
Born: 08/31/86   Age: 32   Bats: R   Throws: R
Height: 6'4"   Weight: 252   Origin: International Free Agent, 2006

YEAR	TEAM	LVL	AGE	W	L	SV	G	GS	IP	H	HR	BB/9	K/9	K	GB%	BABIP
2016	PIT	MLB	29	10	7	0	52	12	118	117	15	3.4	10.5	138	45%	.331
2017	PIT	MLB	30	2	5	2	65	0	60	49	4	2.7	9.0	60	47%	.285
2017	PHI	MLB	30	1	0	0	2	0	1¹	0	0	0.0	6.8	1	100%	.000
2017	SLN	MLB	30	2	0	4	9	0	11	9	1	1.6	9.0	11	39%	.267
2018	SEA	MLB	31	1	6	1	46	0	42	53	6	1.1	11.4	53	37%	.402
2019	PHI	MLB	32	2	2	0	36	0	38	35	5	3.1	10.4	44	42%	.303

Breakout: 25%   Improve: 49%   Collapse: 22%   Attrition: 3%   MLB: 90%
Comparables: Jakie May, Manny Parra, Luke Hochevar

There's one every year, and Nicasio may just have been 2018's King of Small Sample Size Weirdness. Signed to a two-year deal to provide a bridge to Edwin Diaz, Nicasio's peripheral results were exactly what you would hope. He struck out batters at a fast rate than he ever had, and walked fewer. Unfortunately for Nicasio and pitchers everywhere, as long as hitters continue to be pests and not strike out 100% of the time, there will always be balls in play, and when the ball is in play wacky things can happen. In this case, for Nicasio and the Mariners, "wacky" was a bit like Wile E. Coyote with a stick of dynamite. The strength of his velocity and track record of success says that we should expect positive regression in 2019, and if so he can still be a highly effective bridge-inning reliever. If not, well, most people like rooting for the Road Runner anyway.

YEAR	TEAM	LVL	AGE	WHIP	ERA	DRA	WARP	MPH	FB%	WHF	CSP
2016	PIT	MLB	29	1.37	4.50	3.94	1.7	97.2	69.2	11.4	46.1
2017	PIT	MLB	30	1.12	2.85	3.63	1.0	97.3	72.8	12	51.5
2017	PHI	MLB	30	0.00	0.00	5.22	0.0	98.3	45	20	59.7
2017	SLN	MLB	30	1.00	1.64	4.12	0.1	97.6	71.7	13.4	50.3
2018	SEA	MLB	31	1.38	6.00	2.73	1.1	96.0	70.7	12.2	51
2019	PHI	MLB	32	1.27	3.82	4.07	0.3	96.0	69.9	11.8	49.5

Juan Nicasio, continued

Pitch Shape vs LHH

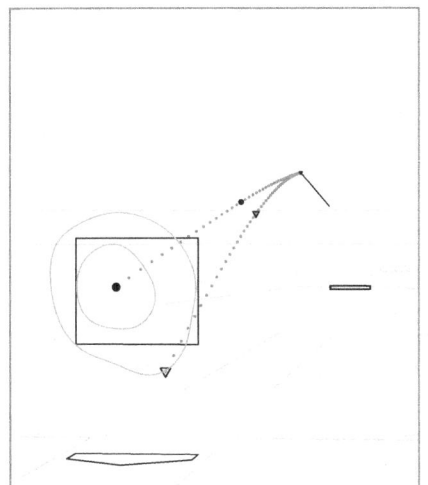

Pitch Shape vs RHH

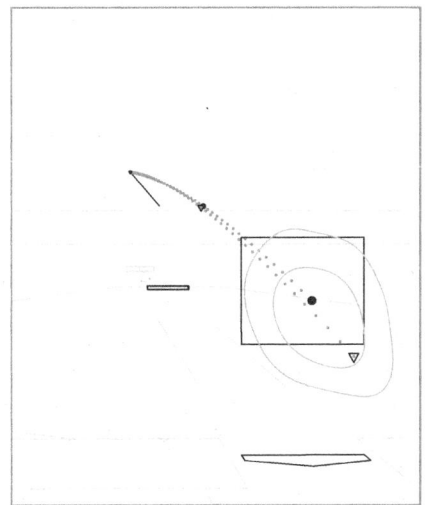

Type	Frequency	Velocity	H Movement	V Movement
● Fastball	70.7%	94.2 [106]	-8 [94]	-13.3 [108]
☐ Sinker				
+ Cutter				
▲ Changeup	0.8%	88.1 [111]	-6.8 [124]	-19.5 [123]
× Splitter				
▽ Slider	28.5%	87.9 [116]	1.7 [86]	-26.2 [120]
◇ Curveball				
✦ Slow Curveball				
✳ Knuckleball				
▼ Screwball				

Aaron Nola RHP

Born: 06/04/93 Age: 26 Bats: R Throws: R
Height: 6'2" Weight: 195 Origin: Round 1, 2014 Draft (#7 overall)

YEAR	TEAM	LVL	AGE	W	L	SV	G	GS	IP	H	HR	BB/9	K/9	K	GB%	BABIP
2016	PHI	MLB	23	6	9	0	20	20	111	116	10	2.4	9.8	121	57%	.334
2017	LEH	AAA	24	1	0	0	2	2	10^1	6	0	0.9	8.7	10	65%	.231
2017	PHI	MLB	24	12	11	0	27	27	168	154	18	2.6	9.9	184	50%	.309
2018	PHI	MLB	25	17	6	0	33	33	212^1	149	17	2.5	9.5	224	52%	.251
2019	PHI	MLB	26	14	8	0	30	30	189	155	17	2.5	10.1	213	51%	.288

Breakout: 21% Improve: 65% Collapse: 17% Attrition: 6% MLB: 95%
Comparables: Jon Lester, Gerrit Cole, Marcus Stroman

Nola made The Leap, the fabled ascendance from "nice player" to "star" that so many yearn for and few achieve. Finally healthy for a full season, Nola sliced his opponents' HR rates and regularly drew poor contact when he wasn't striking guys out. That middle point is crucial, given how notoriously poor the 2018 Phillies were at playing defense, and Nola certainly did his part to make their jobs that much easier. It also helps the bullpen to know that Nola is becoming "Opener"-proof: The .540 OPS he allowed on the third time through the order was second only to Seattle's James Paxton in all of baseball, among pitchers who faced 150-plus batters for the third time. Some might say this version of Nola was lurking all along, shrouded by misleading ERAs that didn't tell the full story. Either way, he'll turn 26 in June, and the best still may be yet to come.

YEAR	TEAM	LVL	AGE	WHIP	ERA	DRA	WARP	MPH	FB%	WHF	CSP
2016	PHI	MLB	23	1.31	4.78	2.74	3.3	93.0	57.7	10.4	48.1
2017	LEH	AAA	24	0.68	0.87	3.48	0.3				
2017	PHI	MLB	24	1.21	3.54	3.22	4.4	94.1	53.3	11.8	49.1
2018	PHI	MLB	25	0.97	2.37	2.60	6.6	94.7	49.5	13.1	48.4
2019	PHI	MLB	26	1.09	3.14	3.28	3.9	93.9	53.1	12.4	49.4

Aaron Nola, continued

Pitch Shape vs LHH

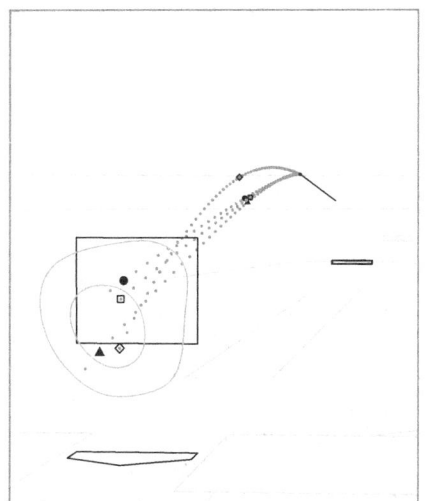

Pitch Shape vs RHH

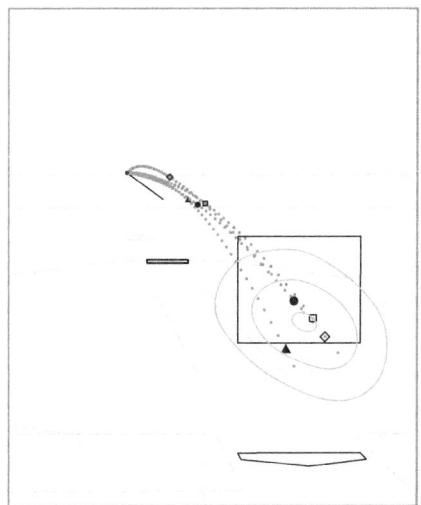

Type	Frequency	Velocity	H Movement	V Movement
● Fastball	35.5%	93.3 [103]	-10.8 [81]	-16.8 [97]
□ Sinker	14.0%	91.9 [97]	-14.7 [83]	-22.4 [93]
+ Cutter				
▲ Changeup	19.6%	85.3 [100]	-12.5 [93]	-32.2 [86]
× Splitter				
▽ Slider				
◇ Curveball	30.9%	78.5 [100]	15.2 [131]	-49.6 [97]
⊕ Slow Curveball				
✳ Knuckleball				
▼ Screwball				

James Pazos LHP

Born: 05/05/91 Age: 28 Bats: R Throws: L
Height: 6'2" Weight: 235 Origin: Round 13, 2012 Draft (#427 overall)

YEAR	TEAM	LVL	AGE	W	L	SV	G	GS	IP	H	HR	BB/9	K/9	K	GB%	BABIP
2016	SWB	AAA	25	2	2	1	23	0	27^1	19	1	6.3	13.5	41	57%	.316
2016	NYA	MLB	25	1	0	0	7	0	3^1	7	2	2.7	8.1	3	46%	.455
2017	SEA	MLB	26	4	5	0	59	0	53^2	51	7	4.0	10.9	65	51%	.317
2018	SEA	MLB	27	4	1	0	60	0	50	47	4	2.7	8.1	45	47%	.303
2019	PHI	MLB	28	2	2	0	41	0	43	41	6	4.3	9.6	47	47%	.297

Breakout: 26% Improve: 44% Collapse: 19% Attrition: 23% MLB: 83%
Comparables: Evan Meek, Zach Putnam, Brandon Medders

The velocity gains that helped vault Pazos to the majors largely disappeared in 2018, but his effectiveness did not. Although his fastball-slider arsenal and track record appear to peg him as a LOOGY, the Mariners actually let Pazos face significantly more right-handers than left last year, and he responded by running significant reverse-splits. While that result is probably more statistical oddity than predictive of future results, and his stuff and command are not close to elite in the modern game, Pazos can now boast a mid-90s fastball and a two-year track record of stable, dependable, big league production. Lengthy careers can and have been made on far less. He's also a reliever, so he could be out of baseball in 24 months.

YEAR	TEAM	LVL	AGE	WHIP	ERA	DRA	WARP	MPH	FB%	WHF	CSP
2016	SWB	AAA	25	1.39	2.63	2.74	0.7				
2016	NYA	MLB	25	2.40	13.50	7.70	-0.1	97.9	65.5	12.1	47.6
2017	SEA	MLB	26	1.40	3.86	3.75	0.9	97.5	74.1	13.1	49.3
2018	SEA	MLB	27	1.24	2.88	4.66	0.2	96.4	91.8	10.8	52.3
2019	PHI	MLB	28	1.41	4.75	4.82	0.0	96.3	83.4	12	50.4

James Pazos, continued

Pitch Shape vs LHH

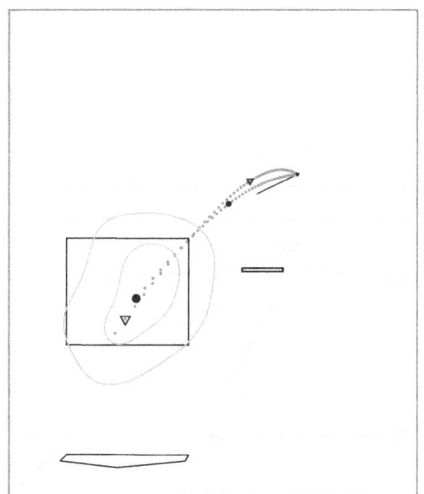

Pitch Shape vs RHH

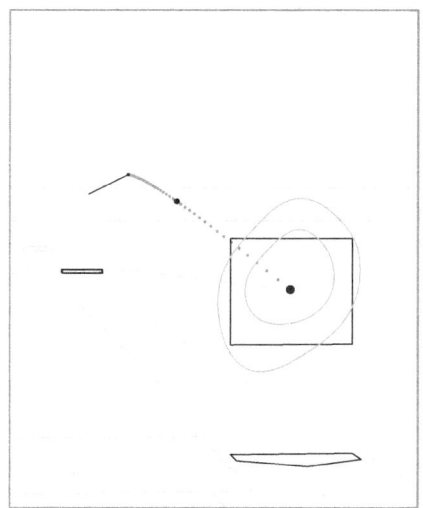

Type		Frequency	Velocity	H Movement	V Movement
●	Fastball	91.8%	94.2 [106]	11.4 [78]	-16.5 [98]
□	Sinker				
+	Cutter				
▲	Changeup				
×	Splitter				
▽	Slider	8.2%	79.5 [78]	-3.3 [93]	-41.3 [75]
◇	Curveball				
✦	Slow Curveball				
✳	Knuckleball				
▼	Screwball				

Nick Pivetta RHP
Born: 02/14/93   Age: 26   Bats: R   Throws: R
Height: 6'5"   Weight: 220   Origin: Round 4, 2013 Draft (#136 overall)

YEAR	TEAM	LVL	AGE	W	L	SV	G	GS	IP	H	HR	BB/9	K/9	K	GB%	BABIP
2016	REA	AA	23	11	6	0	22	22	124	108	10	3.0	8.1	111	45%	.283
2016	LEH	AAA	23	1	2	0	5	5	24²	20	2	3.6	9.9	27	48%	.300
2017	LEH	AAA	24	5	0	0	5	5	32	25	1	0.6	10.4	37	40%	.293
2017	PHI	MLB	24	8	10	0	26	26	133	144	25	3.9	9.5	140	45%	.332
2018	PHI	MLB	25	7	14	0	33	32	164	163	24	2.8	10.3	188	50%	.327
2019	PHI	MLB	26	10	7	0	26	26	148	128	16	2.9	10.2	168	45%	.297

Breakout: 27%   Improve: 46%   Collapse: 14%   Attrition: 16%   MLB: 89%
Comparables: Felipe Paulino, Boof Bonser, Justin Grimm

The Phillies' legendarily poor defense in 2018 probably hurt no single pitcher more than Pivetta, whose peripherals bordered on outstanding while his key traditionals—W/L, ERA, opponents' AVG—provided a mediocre back of a baseball card. Cases like these make it difficult at the surface to explain why Pivetta actually made massive improvements over his rough 2017—a 2017 that, by the way, was also better than a 6.02 ERA would lead you to believe. But this sort of profile is exactly the type of thing you expect to see on lists of breakout candidates: Mid-90s heat, exceptional curveball, an improving change, and a hard slider for a show-me Plan D if all else fails. All of that sure seemed like it meshed well enough for stretches that 2018 should have been the foretold breakout year, but that peskily porous defense and seemingly every mistake pitch not just getting hit but *crushed* kept a lid on that breakout talk. Still, the stuff, body frame, and durability keep hope alive that Pivetta is more than just a back-end innings eater, and maybe 2019 is the season that finally transforms that belief into truth.

YEAR	TEAM	LVL	AGE	WHIP	ERA	DRA	WARP	MPH	FB%	WHF	CSP
2016	REA	AA	23	1.20	3.41	3.43	2.5				
2016	LEH	AAA	23	1.22	2.55	3.87	0.4				
2017	LEH	AAA	24	0.84	1.41	3.22	0.9				
2017	PHI	MLB	24	1.51	6.02	4.66	1.4	96.5	66	10.1	50.2
2018	PHI	MLB	25	1.30	4.77	3.40	3.6	96.6	58.9	13.2	49.1
2019	PHI	MLB	26	1.19	3.48	3.65	2.4	96.2	62.9	12.1	50.5

Nick Pivetta, continued

Pitch Shape vs LHH

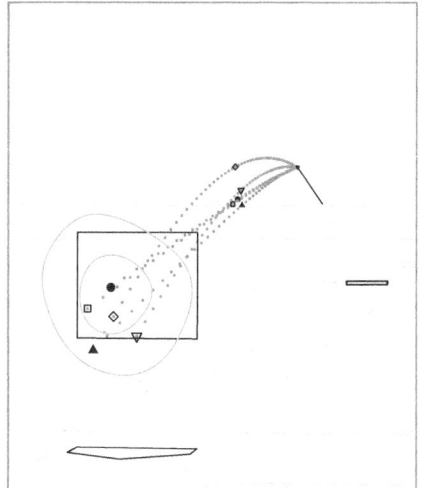

Pitch Shape vs RHH

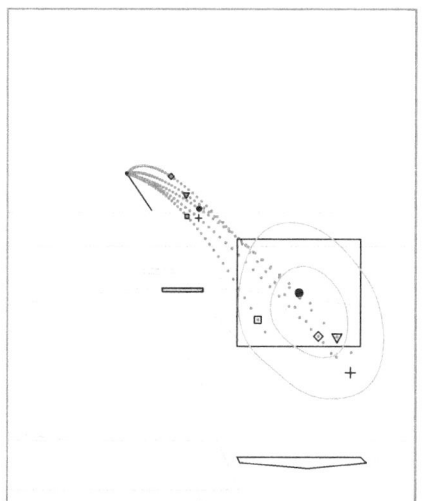

Type	Frequency	Velocity	H Movement	V Movement
● Fastball	52.5%	95.4 [109]	-7.8 [95]	-11.7 [113]
☐ Sinker	6.4%	95.3 [114]	-11.7 [108]	-14.6 [119]
+ Cutter	1.3%	89.5 [104]	3.7 [111]	-24.6 [97]
▲ Changeup	2.3%	87.7 [110]	-12.7 [92]	-24.1 [110]
✕ Splitter				
▽ Slider	15.7%	85.2 [103]	7.7 [112]	-34.4 [96]
◇ Curveball	21.8%	80.6 [108]	11.9 [117]	-50.5 [94]
⊕ Slow Curveball				
✳ Knuckleball				
▼ Screwball				

Philadelphia Phillies 2019

Edubray Ramos RHP
Born: 12/19/92   Age: 26   Bats: R   Throws: R
Height: 6'0"   Weight: 160   Origin: International Free Agent, 2010

YEAR	TEAM	LVL	AGE	W	L	SV	G	GS	IP	H	HR	BB/9	K/9	K	GB%	BABIP
2016	REA	AA	23	1	1	7	11	0	15	9	1	0.6	9.0	15	51%	.211
2016	LEH	AAA	23	1	0	3	15	0	23^2	15	0	1.1	9.9	26	32%	.250
2016	PHI	MLB	23	1	3	0	42	0	40	36	5	2.5	9.0	40	38%	.298
2017	LEH	AAA	24	2	0	1	10	0	11^2	7	0	3.1	7.7	10	38%	.219
2017	PHI	MLB	24	2	7	0	59	0	57^2	57	4	4.4	11.7	75	39%	.356
2018	LEH	AAA	25	0	0	0	6	0	6	8	1	1.5	7.5	5	26%	.389
2018	PHI	MLB	25	3	1	1	52	0	42^2	34	4	3.2	8.9	42	34%	.268
2019	PHI	MLB	26	2	2	0	31	0	32	30	5	3.7	9.6	35	38%	.294

Breakout: 27%   Improve: 41%   Collapse: 25%   Attrition: 22%   MLB: 81%
Comparables: Clay Zavada, Manny Delcarmen, Cam Bedrosian

Through June, Ramos was having a true shutdown season: ERA just above 1.00, opponents OPSing below .600, and everything looking hunky-dory. Then, a wave of injuries crashed on his shores, and Ramos's performance began to wobble. First, a shoulder impingement at the end of June; then, a patella tendon strain in late July; finally, a blister in late August. Over the season's final three months, Ramos was still effective as he pitched through and around his nagging injuries. He remains a touch too generous with the free passes, but has proven himself to be reliable in late-game pressure situations...at least in the ones that don't involve Asdrubal Cabrera. When he's pitching on healthy legs and with unblistered fingers, he'll find most of his success on the back of a sharply-humped low-to-mid-80s slider that can divebomb out of the bottom of the zone.

YEAR	TEAM	LVL	AGE	WHIP	ERA	DRA	WARP	MPH	FB%	WHF	CSP
2016	REA	AA	23	0.67	2.40	2.65	0.4				
2016	LEH	AAA	23	0.76	0.38	2.78	0.6				
2016	PHI	MLB	23	1.17	3.83	4.80	0.1	98.0	53.8	11.8	51.4
2017	LEH	AAA	24	0.94	1.54	2.49	0.4				
2017	PHI	MLB	24	1.47	4.21	4.00	0.8	96.2	42.2	12.2	48.3
2018	LEH	AAA	25	1.50	9.00	6.15	-0.1				
2018	PHI	MLB	25	1.15	2.32	4.54	0.2	95.1	38.2	11.2	48.6
2019	PHI	MLB	26	1.32	4.47	4.60	0.1	95.8	43.6	11.9	50

Edubray Ramos, continued

Pitch Shape vs LHH

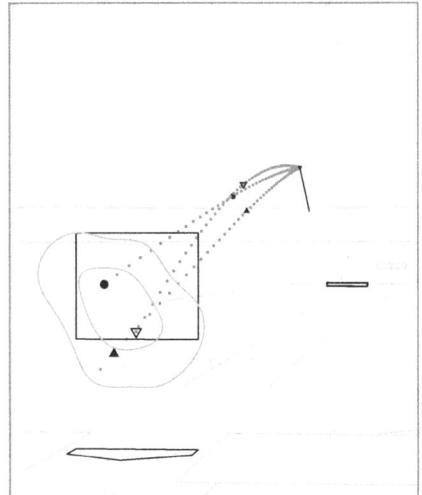

Pitch Shape vs RHH

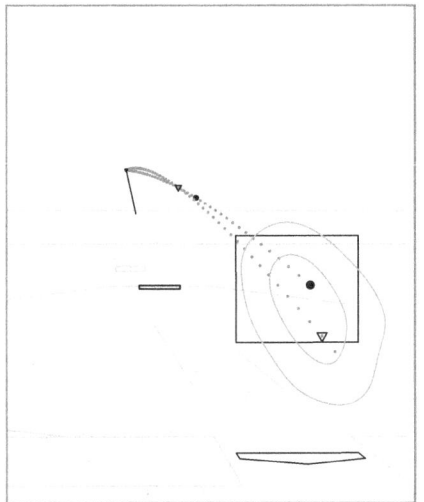

Type	Frequency	Velocity	H Movement	V Movement
● Fastball	35.1%	93.8 [104]	-3.8 [113]	-15.2 [102]
□ Sinker	3.1%	91.8 [97]	-12.4 [102]	-21.4 [97]
+ Cutter				
▲ Changeup	4.5%	89 [114]	-11.2 [101]	-21.9 [116]
× Splitter				
▽ Slider	56.8%	83.4 [95]	8.9 [118]	-37.8 [86]
◇ Curveball	0.5%	79.9 [105]	4.9 [88]	-44 [109]
⊕ Slow Curveball				
✳ Knuckleball				
▼ Screwball				

Philadelphia Phillies 2019

Yacksel Rios RHP
Born: 06/27/93   Age: 26   Bats: R   Throws: R
Height: 6'3"   Weight: 185   Origin: Round 12, 2011 Draft (#391 overall)

YEAR	TEAM	LVL	AGE	W	L	SV	G	GS	IP	H	HR	BB/9	K/9	K	GB%	BABIP
2016	REA	AA	23	1	1	0	13	1	17^2	20	0	7.1	10.7	21	47%	.392
2016	CLR	A+	23	4	3	1	22	6	58^2	59	4	3.5	6.4	42	44%	.306
2017	REA	AA	24	1	2	2	24	0	38	22	2	2.4	11.1	47	40%	.235
2017	LEH	AAA	24	0	1	1	13	1	18^1	10	3	2.0	8.3	17	36%	.159
2017	PHI	MLB	24	1	0	0	13	0	16^1	15	4	5.0	9.4	17	36%	.256
2018	LEH	AAA	25	0	0	1	22	0	22^2	18	2	6.8	10.3	26	54%	.281
2018	PHI	MLB	25	3	2	0	36	0	36	43	6	3.8	9.0	36	47%	.349
2019	PHI	MLB	26	1	0	0	10	0	11	10	1	4.6	9.5	12	44%	.293

Breakout: 15%   Improve: 25%   Collapse: 5%   Attrition: 16%   MLB: 38%
Comparables: Mayckol Guaipe, Lucas Luetge, Randor Bierd

Somewhere in the 2017-18 offseason, Rios must have unearthed some sort of enchanted totem or magic lamp that allowed him to add four MPH to his fastball, an overnight bump from 93-94 to 97 with semi-regular touches of 99 and 100. As we've all seen, however, pure raw velo does not a pitcher make. Rios is clearly more powerful now, but that doesn't mean he was overwhelming opposing hitters as a result. For what it's worth, Rios's new cannon delivers this enhanced heat with as much ease as his old 93-94 MPH self, and his slider vexed plenty of right-handed hitters. His bugaboo pretty clearly remains left-handed batters, though, and any hope of hanging on to a bullpen role lies pretty squarely on improving his splitter and locating his fastball better when attacking them.

YEAR	TEAM	LVL	AGE	WHIP	ERA	DRA	WARP	MPH	FB%	WHF	CSP
2016	REA	AA	23	1.92	4.58	2.80	0.4				
2016	CLR	A+	23	1.40	6.14	3.75	1.0				
2017	REA	AA	24	0.84	1.89	3.02	0.8				
2017	LEH	AAA	24	0.76	1.96	3.25	0.4				
2017	PHI	MLB	24	1.47	4.41	6.52	-0.2	95.6	64.1	11.6	48.3
2018	LEH	AAA	25	1.54	3.97	4.33	0.2				
2018	PHI	MLB	25	1.61	6.75	4.14	0.3	98.6	64.3	12.2	48.6
2019	PHI	MLB	26	1.40	4.49	4.61	0.0	97.4	65.4	12.3	49.3

Yacksel Rios, continued

Pitch Shape vs LHH

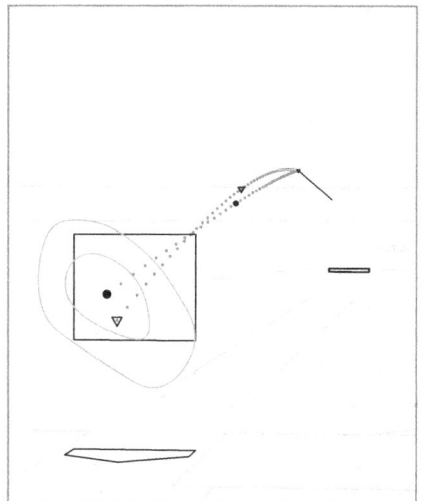

Pitch Shape vs RHH

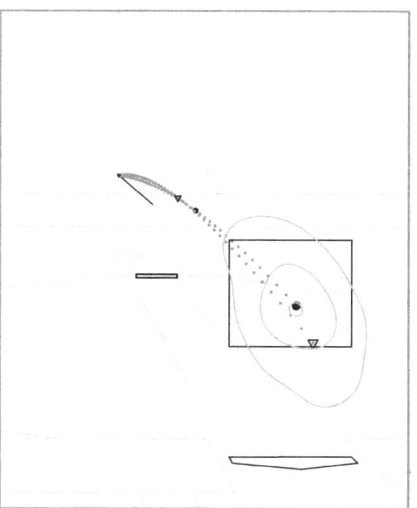

Type	Frequency	Velocity	H Movement	V Movement
● Fastball	64.3%	96.5 [113]	-11.1 [79]	-15.2 [102]
□ Sinker				
+ Cutter				
▲ Changeup				
× Splitter	3.2%	84.8 [95]	-4.2 [115]	-32 [89]
▽ Slider	32.5%	86.4 [109]	1.1 [84]	-32.1 [103]
◇ Curveball				
✦ Slow Curveball				
✳ Knuckleball				
▼ Screwball				

David Robertson   RHP

Born: 04/09/85   Age: 34   Bats: R   Throws: R
Height: 5'11"   Weight: 195   Origin: Round 17, 2006 Draft (#524 overall)

YEAR	TEAM	LVL	AGE	W	L	SV	G	GS	IP	H	HR	BB/9	K/9	K	GB%	BABIP
2016	CHA	MLB	31	5	3	37	62	0	62^1	53	6	4.6	10.8	75	47%	.307
2017	CHA	MLB	32	4	2	13	31	0	33^1	21	4	3.0	12.7	47	43%	.250
2017	NYA	MLB	32	5	0	1	30	0	35	14	2	3.1	13.1	51	56%	.182
2018	NYA	MLB	33	8	3	5	69	0	69^2	46	7	3.4	11.8	91	47%	.245
2019	PHI	MLB	34	3	2	14	52	0	54	43	6	3.9	11.3	69	46%	.287

Breakout: 14%   Improve: 28%   Collapse: 46%   Attrition: 7%   MLB: 94%
Comparables: Seung Hwan Oh, Darren O'Day, J.J. Putz

This decade, only two relievers have more Win Probability Added than David Robertson: Kenley Jansen and Craig Kimbrel. Dig further: Robertson's average Leverage Index upon entering the game is always lower than those two; he played behind Mariano Rivera to start his career, then as a closer on an underperforming White Sox crew, and now he is a relief ace among many. What's even more remarkable than his career numbers is the sheer consistency of it all. Here are things he has done in every single season since 2010: pitched more than 60 innings, struck out at least ten batters per nine innings, and allowed fewer than one home run per nine innings. Even he knows it: for the first time in his career, he represented himself in free agency, stating in a self-penned letter to MLB Trade Rumors that he "know[s] what [he] can offer a team." We do too—just look at his baseball card.

YEAR	TEAM	LVL	AGE	WHIP	ERA	DRA	WARP	MPH	FB%	WHF	CSP
2016	CHA	MLB	31	1.36	3.47	2.57	1.7	94.5	68.1	13.7	45.6
2017	CHA	MLB	32	0.96	2.70	1.98	1.2	93.2	56.1	16.5	46.9
2017	NYA	MLB	32	0.74	1.03	1.86	1.3	93.7	56.1	18.4	43.2
2018	NYA	MLB	33	1.03	3.23	3.03	1.5	94.1	42.5	14.4	43.3
2019	PHI	MLB	34	1.22	3.34	3.68	0.7	92.8	52	14.9	43.8

David Robertson, continued

Pitch Shape vs LHH

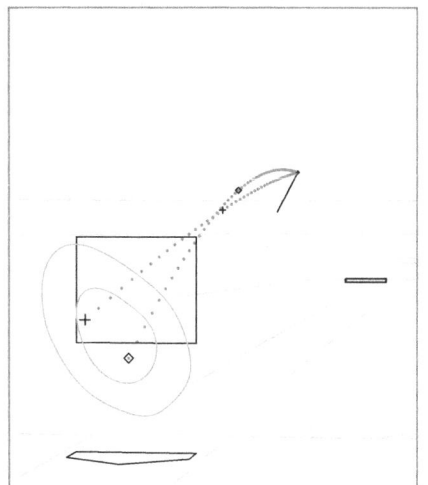

Pitch Shape vs RHH

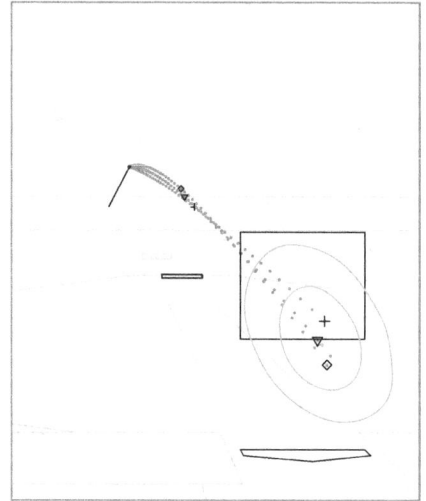

Type	Frequency	Velocity	H Movement	V Movement
● Fastball				
□ Sinker	0.9%	94.1 [108]	-12.6 [100]	-16 [114]
+ Cutter	41.6%	92.6 [123]	2.3 [103]	-14.2 [138]
▲ Changeup	0.3%	88.5 [113]	-14.7 [82]	-22.6 [114]
× Splitter				
▽ Slider	9.9%	86.9 [111]	7.4 [111]	-30.7 [107]
◇ Curveball	47.4%	84.3 [122]	9.3 [106]	-43.2 [111]
⊕ Slow Curveball				
✳ Knuckleball				
▼ Screwball				

Ranger Suarez LHP

Born: 08/26/95 Age: 23 Bats: L Throws: L
Height: 6'1" Weight: 180 Origin: International Free Agent, 2012

YEAR	TEAM	LVL	AGE	W	L	SV	G	GS	IP	H	HR	BB/9	K/9	K	GB%	BABIP
2016	WPT	A-	20	6	4	0	13	13	73^2	61	4	2.9	6.5	53	53%	.260
2017	LWD	A	21	6	2	0	14	14	85	52	4	2.5	9.5	90	58%	.233
2017	CLR	A+	21	2	4	0	8	8	37^2	43	1	2.6	9.1	38	50%	.382
2018	REA	AA	22	4	3	0	12	12	75	64	2	2.4	6.5	54	51%	.283
2018	LEH	AAA	22	2	0	0	9	9	49^1	48	2	2.7	5.7	31	50%	.297
2018	PHI	MLB	22	1	1	0	4	3	15	21	3	3.6	6.6	11	52%	.367
2019	PHI	MLB	23	2	2	0	6	6	30	31	5	3.3	7.6	25	46%	.293

Breakout: 16% Improve: 20% Collapse: 10% Attrition: 27% MLB: 41%
Comparables: Troy Patton, Michael Bowden, Jorge Lopez

When he made his Major League debut on July 26, Suarez snapped one of the most peculiar streaks in all of baseball: The Phillies, as a team, had not had a left-handed pitcher start a game since Adam Morgan in late September 2016. Further, Suarez was the first lefty younger than 24 to start for the Fightins since Antonio Bastardo way back in 2009. In that way, Suarez is emblematic of an organizational deficiency that lasted for years and is only just now being rectified as some starting southpaws finally claw their way through the system. He's unlikely to draw any Cole Hamels comparisons, and the vanishing of his strikeouts from 2017 to 2018 is borderline alarming, but Suarez, by all accounts, isn't done improving. He's consistently added velocity since coming to the U.S. in 2015, features a strong changeup to offset his low-90s fastball, and has made strides to sharpen his curveball. If that curve continues to get better and solidifies itself as a legitimate third pitch in Suarez's arsenal, there's something more than just "viable" at work here. There's still a good distance between that future and the present, but expect Suarez to get his fair shake of chances to have it all come together.

YEAR	TEAM	LVL	AGE	WHIP	ERA	DRA	WARP	MPH	FB%	WHF	CSP
2016	WPT	A-	20	1.15	2.81	3.62	1.4				
2017	LWD	A	21	0.89	1.59	3.05	2.2				
2017	CLR	A+	21	1.43	3.82	3.76	0.7				
2018	REA	AA	22	1.12	2.76	4.71	0.6				
2018	LEH	AAA	22	1.28	2.74	4.02	0.9				
2018	PHI	MLB	22	1.80	5.40	5.73	-0.1	93.7	60.4	7.6	51.1
2019	PHI	MLB	23	1.36	4.85	5.12	0.0	93.6	62.6	7.8	53

Ranger Suarez, continued

Pitch Shape vs LHH

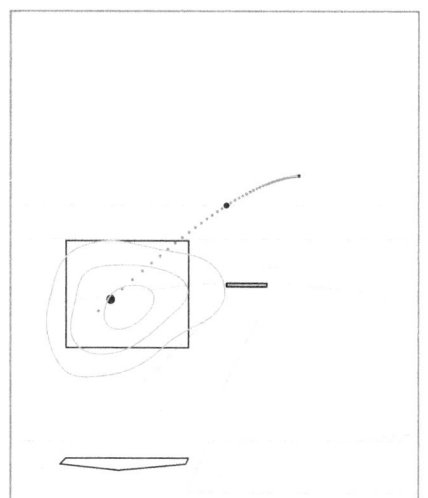

Pitch Shape vs RHH

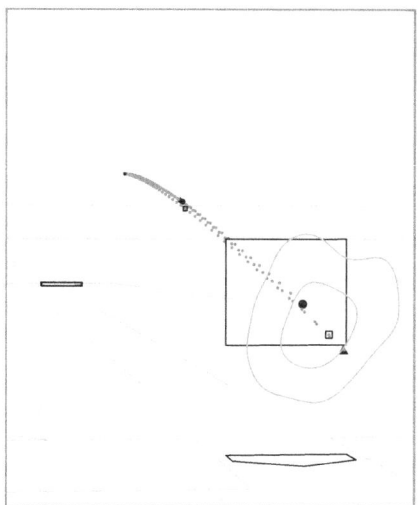

Type		Frequency	Velocity	H Movement	V Movement
●	Fastball	37.3%	92.9 [101]	4.3 [111]	-17.9 [93]
☐	Sinker	23.1%	91.4 [95]	13.2 [95]	-24.3 [87]
+	Cutter				
▲	Changeup	20.4%	84.7 [98]	11.2 [101]	-28.9 [95]
✕	Splitter				
▽	Slider	19.1%	82.4 [91]	-5.9 [105]	-33.2 [99]
◇	Curveball				
⊕	Slow Curveball				
✱	Knuckleball				
▼	Screwball				

Phillies Player Analysis - 87

Vincent Velasquez RHP
Born: 06/07/92 Age: 27 Bats: R Throws: R
Height: 6'3" Weight: 205 Origin: Round 2, 2010 Draft (#58 overall)

YEAR	TEAM	LVL	AGE	W	L	SV	G	GS	IP	H	HR	BB/9	K/9	K	GB%	BABIP
2016	PHI	MLB	24	8	6	0	24	24	131	129	21	3.1	10.4	152	37%	.325
2017	PHI	MLB	25	2	7	0	15	15	72	74	15	4.2	8.5	68	45%	.303
2018	PHI	MLB	26	9	12	0	31	30	146²	138	16	3.6	9.9	161	41%	.316
2019	PHI	MLB	27	6	6	0	32	16	96	88	14	3.5	10.0	108	41%	.299

Breakout: 33% Improve: 64% Collapse: 18% Attrition: 12% MLB: 93%
Comparables: Ian Snell, Max Scherzer, Mike Minor

Give Velasquez this: He had the conditioning to make 30 starts (plus one relief appearance) for the first time. Now, those starts were severely abbreviated—VV became the first pitcher ever to reach that mark throwing fewer than 150 innings—so we're no closer to understanding if Velasquez can really hack it as a SP or not. We're now roughly four years deep into this exploration, rapidly approaching the point of no return, and the only thing getting clearer is the worry that simply shifting Velasquez to a relief role won't fix what ails him. Does he still throw hard? Sure. But erratic command and gopheritis aren't things that typically get fixed simply by letting a guy throw harder for a shorter (on purpose, in this scenario) amount of time. It's still pretty plain that Velasquez has a top-tier arm, but no coach in Philadelphia has, thus far, been able to help him fully harness its capabilities for more than a scattered start here or there. It's not for lack of effort, nor work ethic, nor athleticism—I mean, did you *see* him get hit by a liner and recover to throw a bullet to first with his *left hand* to record the out?!—but something just isn't working. The Phillies figure to give him another look in 2019, but he may find himself in another uniform soon.

YEAR	TEAM	LVL	AGE	WHIP	ERA	DRA	WARP	MPH	FB%	WHF	CSP
2016	PHI	MLB	24	1.33	4.12	3.54	2.7	96.8	64.9	12.7	49.1
2017	PHI	MLB	25	1.50	5.12	5.66	-0.1	96.2	68.5	10.1	51.7
2018	PHI	MLB	26	1.34	4.85	4.20	1.9	96.2	64	12.5	50.3
2019	PHI	MLB	27	1.31	4.17	4.39	0.7	95.9	66	12.2	51.1

Vincent Velasquez, continued

Pitch Shape vs LHH

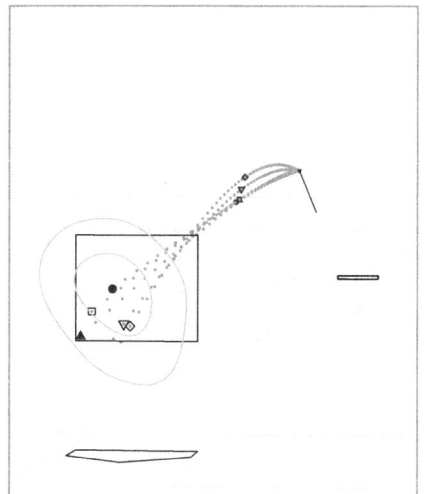

Pitch Shape vs RHH

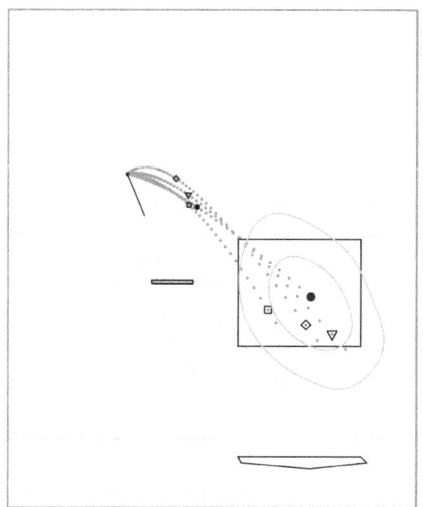

Type	Frequency	Velocity	H Movement	V Movement
● Fastball	54.4%	94.6 [107]	-3.5 [115]	-12.2 [111]
☐ Sinker	9.6%	93.2 [103]	-11.8 [107]	-20.8 [99]
+ Cutter				
▲ Changeup	5.4%	88.9 [114]	-11 [102]	-25.1 [107]
× Splitter				
▽ Slider	16.1%	85.3 [104]	4.5 [98]	-33.5 [99]
◇ Curveball	14.4%	81.8 [112]	5.9 [92]	-46.5 [104]
✦ Slow Curveball				
✳ Knuckleball				
▼ Screwball				

Alec Bohm 3B

Born: 08/03/96 Age: 22 Bats: R Throws: R
Height: 6'5" Weight: 225 Origin: Round 1, 2018 Draft (#3 overall)

YEAR	TEAM	LVL	AGE	PA	R	2B	3B	HR	RBI	BB	K	SB	CS	AVG/OBP/SLG
2018	WPT	A-	21	121	9	5	1	0	12	10	19	1	0	.224/.314/.290
2019	PHI	MLB	22	251	15	5	0	5	21	9	68	0	0	.122/.160/.210

Breakout: 1% Improve: 1% Collapse: 0% Attrition: 1% MLB: 1%
Comparables: Ryder Jones, Kaleb Cowart, Mitch Walding

If you follow sports besides baseball and, deeper still, the Philadelphia teams within, you'll probably sense the comparisons about to come here. For those uninitiated, allow me to present a quick primer. Top Philly draftees, across all sports, have kicked off their careers in Philadelphia by being hurt within a year or so. From Joel Embiid and Ben Simmons with the 76ers to Carson Wentz with the Eagles to seemingly anybody who tries to play goalie for the Flyers, dudes just seem to get banged up right as they're getting started in their new home. Which brings us to Bohm, the third overall pick in the 2018 Draft out of Wichita State, who made it roughly three weeks before getting plunked in the knee by a pitch and missing a month. It *felt* inevitable. The good news is that Bohm made it back before the end of the season, a welcome divergence from the tales of Embiid, Simmons, and Jones. The crystal ball forecasts Bohm as a contact/power combo that's becoming more and more rare in this age of baseball, and though he didn't hit for a ton of power in his pro debut, there seems to be little doubt he could poke 20-plus homers with an average in the .300 area and, probably, garner some All-Star votes along the way. If he can make all of that work while sticking at third base, the Phillies may finally have the hot corner mainstay they've been in search of for so many years.

YEAR	TEAM	LVL	AGE	PA	DRC+	VORP	BABIP	BRR	FRAA	WARP
2018	WPT	A-	21	121	90	-0.4	.273	-0.9	3B(20): -2.7	-0.6
2019	PHI	MLB	22	251	-7	-27.1	.144	-0.4	3B -1	-3.0

Luis Garcia SS

Born: 10/01/00 Age: 18 Bats: B Throws: R
Height: 5'11" Weight: 170 Origin: International Free Agent, 2017

YEAR	TEAM	LVL	AGE	PA	R	2B	3B	HR	RBI	BB	K	SB	CS	AVG/OBP/SLG
2018	PLL	RK	17	187	33	11	3	1	32	15	21	12	8	.369/.433/.488
2019	PHI	MLB	18	251	25	8	0	4	19	3	61	5	3	.224/.231/.309

Comparables: Adalberto Mondesi, Wilmer Flores, Tommy Brown

No, no, not *that* **Luis Garcia**. This is a new one, and he plays shortstop. The Phillies signed Garcia with $2.5 million of their pool money in July 2017, and if a club with a history of finding diamonds in the rough for a fraction of that amount goes all-in for multiple millions, you figure they must really like this guy. The switch-hitter produced some satisfying numbers in the Gulf Coast League in 2018, and if he adds a little strength to his relatively lithe 5'11", 170-pound frame, there might even be a teensy bit of power projection to look forward to as he rounds out his teenage years. As it stands, Garcia was regarded as one of the top defenders in his J2 class, and a skilled defensive shortstop will always find a home.

YEAR	TEAM	LVL	AGE	PA	DRC+	VORP	BABIP	BRR	FRAA	WARP
2018	PLL	RK	17	187	197	22.6	.418	-0.1	SS(43): -2.1	1.6
2019	PHI	MLB	18	251	39	-8.8	.277	-0.2	SS -1	-1.1

Adam Haseley OF
Born: 04/12/96   Age: 23   Bats: L   Throws: L
Height: 6'1"   Weight: 195   Origin: Round 1, 2017 Draft (#8 overall)

YEAR	TEAM	LVL	AGE	PA	R	2B	3B	HR	RBI	BB	K	SB	CS	AVG/OBP/SLG
2017	WPT	A-	21	158	18	9	0	2	18	14	28	5	3	.270/.350/.380
2017	LWD	A	21	74	15	3	1	1	6	6	13	0	1	.258/.315/.379
2018	CLR	A+	22	354	54	13	5	5	38	19	54	7	3	.300/.343/.415
2018	REA	AA	22	159	23	4	0	6	17	16	19	0	1	.316/.403/.478
2019	PHI	MLB	23	251	28	7	1	7	25	13	51	1	0	.224/.272/.355

Breakout: 8%   Improve: 20%   Collapse: 0%   Attrition: 8%   MLB: 23%
Comparables: Matt Szczur, Gary Brown, Logan Schafer

Finally! A Phillies position prospect who didn't immediately begin to regress in his second pro year! Haseley's quick movement through the minor leagues has some wondering whether he might force his way into some Major League time later in 2019, though proving himself across more than 159 Double-A PAs has to happen first. With an ability to play any outfield position—LF is probably his best spot, even as the bulk of his starts have come in CF—and minimal platoon splits at the plate, the likes of Aaron Altherr and Nick Williams might be on the clock to show whether they can keep Haseley at arm's length from their share of playing time. Haseley loads like Bryce Harper at the plate, with a follow-through that packs only a portion of the latter's violence, but what he defers in the power department, he makes up for with still-quick hands, good plate coverage, and an ever-improving sense of the strike zone. It allows him to make consistent contact and avoid high-K output, and although that might transform him into something more like Denard Span than Harper, it's hard to find fault with anything that falls between either of those outcomes.

YEAR	TEAM	LVL	AGE	PA	DRC+	VORP	BABIP	BRR	FRAA	WARP
2017	WPT	A-	21	158	129	12.9	.321	2.6	CF(31): 0.1	0.7
2017	LWD	A	21	74	108	6.1	.302	1.6	LF(12): 1.3, CF(4): 0.8	0.5
2018	CLR	A+	22	354	109	15.2	.346	2.9	LF(39): -2.5, CF(30): -2.2	0.7
2018	REA	AA	22	159	133	13.1	.327	-0.5	CF(28): -2.3, LF(5): -0.5	0.4
2019	PHI	MLB	23	251	68	-1.7	.254	-0.3	CF 0, LF 0	-0.2

Mickey Moniak CF

Born: 05/13/98 Age: 21 Bats: L Throws: R
Height: 6'2" Weight: 185 Origin: Round 1, 2016 Draft (#1 overall)

YEAR	TEAM	LVL	AGE	PA	R	2B	3B	HR	RBI	BB	K	SB	CS	AVG/OBP/SLG
2016	PHL	RK	18	194	27	11	4	1	28	11	35	10	4	.284/.340/.409
2017	LWD	A	19	509	53	22	6	5	44	28	109	11	7	.236/.284/.341
2018	CLR	A+	20	465	50	28	3	5	55	22	100	6	5	.270/.304/.383
2019	PHI	MLB	21	251	16	7	1	5	22	2	70	1	1	.164/.172/.259

Breakout: 2% Improve: 2% Collapse: 0% Attrition: 2% MLB: 2%
Comparables: Abraham Almonte, Xavier Avery, Rafael Ortega

On the surface, it looks like Moniak made only slight improvements from 2017 into 2018. You look at the sub-.700 OPS and grimace a little, thinking the former No. 1 overall pick is still falling well short of expectations. But Moniak's year requires a closer look, and upon that further examination, it seems like there's a legitimate reason to be excited about what he can do in 2019. From late May through the end of the season, Moniak slashed .301/.342/.460, dramatically reducing his strikeout rate along the way. He might not be beating down the door for a spot with the Big League club anytime soon, nor is he all that likely to even return to Top Prospect lists heading into '19. But seeing as he doesn't turn 21 until May, it remains far too soon to call him a bust or rule him out of the Phillies' future plans altogether, assuming the adjustments he made from May onward prove sustainable.

YEAR	TEAM	LVL	AGE	PA	DRC+	VORP	BABIP	BRR	FRAA	WARP
2016	PHL	RK	18	194	124	9.0	.345	3.0	CF(30): 4.6, LF(2): 0.1	1.0
2017	LWD	A	19	509	85	13.3	.292	-0.1	CF(115): -9.8	-1.1
2018	CLR	A+	20	465	85	6.6	.334	-0.1	CF(99): -7.3, LF(9): -0.3	-1.1
2019	PHI	MLB	21	251	8	-18.7	.203	-0.3	CF -3, LF 0	-2.3

Jose Pujols RF
Born: 09/29/95   Age: 23   Bats: R   Throws: R
Height: 6'3"   Weight: 175   Origin: International Free Agent, 2012

YEAR	TEAM	LVL	AGE	PA	R	2B	3B	HR	RBI	BB	K	SB	CS	AVG/OBP/SLG
2016	LWD	A	20	549	67	21	3	24	82	44	179	5	3	.241/.306/.440
2017	CLR	A+	21	352	24	10	1	8	29	23	150	2	2	.194/.247/.305
2018	CLR	A+	22	387	56	16	4	18	58	33	127	1	1	.301/.364/.523
2018	REA	AA	22	104	11	2	0	4	18	14	35	2	2	.270/.365/.427
2019	PHI	MLB	23	251	22	5	0	9	28	12	102	1	0	.178/.215/.313

Breakout: 5%   Improve: 10%   Collapse: 1%   Attrition: 8%   MLB: 13%
Comparables: Willy Garcia, Jamie Romak, Dylan Cozens

What makes Pujols's 2018 breakout surprising isn't necessarily that it happened in the first place, but the magnitude by which his numbers jumped. After a washout 2017, Pujols returned to the Florida State League with a steadied hand and improved approach that helped him make more out of the moments he made contact. He still has a long road to travel in that whole "make contact" journey, and it isn't surprising to see so much of his slash line's improvement attributed to a BABIP spike, but things appear to finally be moving in the right direction nonetheless. If he's going to have any shot at the Bigs, it nearly goes without saying that striking out 35 percent of the time at every level has to stop. Even as Pujols was punched out in 35 of his 104 Double-A PAs, though, he nudged his walk rate to the highest point it's ever been, and it's clear there's far more to work with entering a pivotal 2019 than there was at this same point last year. The Phillies slipped him through the Rule 5 Draft once again, but this will be his last chance to prove worthy of a 40-man spot before he accrues enough pro time to hit free agency next offseason.

YEAR	TEAM	LVL	AGE	PA	DRC+	VORP	BABIP	BRR	FRAA	WARP
2016	LWD	A	20	549	114	18.5	.322	-2.7	RF(113): 4.7	0.9
2017	CLR	A+	21	352	56	-11.7	.324	-1.7	RF(63): 1.4, LF(1): -0.2	-1.9
2018	CLR	A+	22	387	151	23.7	.425	-3.0	RF(88): 3.9	2.1
2018	REA	AA	22	104	112	5.0	.392	0.2	RF(24): -2.1, CF(1): -0.2	0.0
2019	PHI	MLB	23	251	38	-12.4	.261	-0.4	RF 1, CF 0	-1.3

Jerad Eickhoff RHP

Born: 07/02/90 Age: 28 Bats: R Throws: R
Height: 6'4" Weight: 245 Origin: Round 15, 2011 Draft (#474 overall)

YEAR	TEAM	LVL	AGE	W	L	SV	G	GS	IP	H	HR	BB/9	K/9	K	GB%	BABIP
2016	PHI	MLB	25	11	14	0	33	33	197^1	187	30	1.9	7.6	167	43%	.278
2017	PHI	MLB	26	4	8	0	24	24	128	142	16	3.7	8.3	118	39%	.328
2018	LEH	AAA	27	0	0	0	4	4	18^2	17	1	3.9	4.8	10	52%	.267
2018	PHI	MLB	27	0	1	0	3	1	5^1	10	1	0.0	18.6	11	20%	.643
2019	PHI	MLB	28	5	5	0	16	16	80	75	10	3.0	8.6	76	42%	.289

Breakout: 21% Improve: 53% Collapse: 10% Attrition: 21% MLB: 89%
Comparables: Chase Anderson, Vidal Nuno, Dan Straily

For a time, it seemed like Eickhoff would be the surprise crown jewel of the Cole Hamels trade: The name no one in Philadelphia recognized in July 2015 eventually turning into one that regularly made starts alongside Aaron Nola for years to come. Would that baseball were that fair. First, it was a strained lat in mid-March. Then, numbness and tingling in the fingers of his pitching hand apparently **not** caused by Thoracic Outlet Syndrome, though the origin remains mostly mysterious. After that, a cortisone shot for his shoulder in June and his right wrist in July, all eventually culminating in a triumphant return to Philadelphia for three September appearances, including eight strikeouts in an abbreviated 3.1-inning start on September 28. For all we know, Eickhoff still has a long road to travel in his recovery. Maybe he never makes 30 starts in a season again. But the trials of 2018 have left little doubt about Eick's determination to get past whatever it is that ails him, and Phillies fans will always appreciate that.

YEAR	TEAM	LVL	AGE	WHIP	ERA	DRA	WARP	MPH	FB%	WHF	CSP
2016	PHI	MLB	25	1.16	3.65	3.83	3.5	93.4	52.8	9.9	46.2
2017	PHI	MLB	26	1.52	4.71	5.24	0.5	92.2	50.2	9.7	48.4
2018	LEH	AAA	27	1.34	2.41	6.78	-0.3				
2018	PHI	MLB	27	1.88	6.75	3.07	0.1	92.0	52	19.4	49
2019	PHI	MLB	28	1.24	4.14	4.36	0.6	92.3	51.8	10.1	48.4

Philadelphia Phillies 2019

Cole Irvin LHP

Born: 01/31/94 Age: 25 Bats: L Throws: L
Height: 6'4" Weight: 180 Origin: Round 5, 2016 Draft (#137 overall)

YEAR	TEAM	LVL	AGE	W	L	SV	G	GS	IP	H	HR	BB/9	K/9	K	GB%	BABIP
2016	WPT	A-	22	5	1	0	10	7	45^2	36	2	1.6	7.3	37	49%	.248
2017	CLR	A+	23	4	6	0	12	11	67	68	2	1.9	7.0	52	55%	.317
2017	REA	AA	23	5	3	0	13	13	84^1	72	12	2.6	7.0	66	46%	.248
2018	LEH	AAA	24	14	4	0	26	25	161^1	135	11	2.0	7.3	131	47%	.270
2019	PHI	MLB	25	8	8	0	22	22	131^2	128	21	2.6	7.6	111	44%	.294

Breakout: 11% Improve: 29% Collapse: 12% Attrition: 31% MLB: 47%
Comparables: Matt Bowman, Taylor Rogers, Simon Castro

It's been a few years now since the last time a Phillies player won a major award at the MLB level, but as far as the International League Pitcher of the Year Award is concerned, they've got that market cornered. Irvin became the latest member of the Phillies organization—the second in three years and sixth since 2001—to take home the crown after posting a sparkling record for the Lehigh Valley IronPigs. The 2016 5th-rounder out of the University of Oregon has been pretty remarkably consistent with his rate stats as a pro, regularly striking out around 17-20 percent while keeping walks and homers to a minimum. Irvin features a four-pitch mix of fastball, change, curve, and slider without a glaring weakness in the bunch, even if none of the four rates out as particularly flashy. He seems like a modest-floor, low-ceiling rotation option who will find his way onto the 40-man roster for the coming season, and a Major League debut won't be too far behind that.

YEAR	TEAM	LVL	AGE	WHIP	ERA	DRA	WARP	MPH	FB%	WHF	CSP
2016	WPT	A-	22	0.96	1.97	2.83	1.3				
2017	CLR	A+	23	1.22	2.55	3.54	1.3				
2017	REA	AA	23	1.14	4.06	4.28	0.9				
2018	LEH	AAA	24	1.05	2.57	3.65	3.4				
2019	PHI	MLB	25	1.26	4.55	5.12	0.3				

Adonis Medina RHP

Born: 12/18/96 Age: 22 Bats: R Throws: R
Height: 6'1" Weight: 185 Origin: International Free Agent, 2014

YEAR	TEAM	LVL	AGE	W	L	SV	G	GS	IP	H	HR	BB/9	K/9	K	GB%	BABIP
2016	WPT	A-	19	5	3	0	13	13	64²	47	5	3.3	4.7	34	57%	.214
2017	LWD	A	20	4	9	0	22	22	119²	103	7	2.9	10.0	133	49%	.306
2018	CLR	A+	21	10	4	0	22	21	111¹	103	11	2.9	9.9	123	51%	.316
2019	*PHI*	*MLB*	*22*	*6*	*6*	*0*	*19*	*19*	*97*	*93*	*13*	*3.9*	*9.0*	*97*	*45%*	*.315*

Breakout: 3%   Improve: 6%   Collapse: 5%   Attrition: 9%   MLB: 13%
Comparables: Anthony Swarzak, Brett Kennedy, John Gant

We may never know if Medina was actually offered to the Baltimore Orioles—or if it was the O's who requested him—for Manny Machado in July. The tricky thing about labels, though, is that they tend to linger, and the label Medina has now been branded with in Philadelphia is "Guy Who Could've Landed Us Machado." Part of the problem is that Medina lacks many other distinctions as a prospect: He climbs rungs and improves his pitches methodically and almost imperceptibly. At his best, Medina will be absolutely overpowering—he had multiple starts with 12 strikeouts and zero walks—but just as easily will be puzzlingly ineffective at his worst. Something is still yet to click for the 22-year-old, and he'll have to figure out what's missing while facing his most advanced opposition yet at Double-A Reading in 2019.

YEAR	TEAM	LVL	AGE	WHIP	ERA	DRA	WARP	MPH	FB%	WHF	CSP
2016	WPT	A-	19	1.10	2.92	3.89	1.0				
2017	LWD	A	20	1.19	3.01	2.93	3.3				
2018	CLR	A+	21	1.25	4.12	4.72	0.8				
2019	*PHI*	*MLB*	*22*	*1.39*	*4.41*	*4.97*	*.0.4*				

JoJo Romero LHP

Born: 09/09/96 Age: 22 Bats: L Throws: L
Height: 6'0" Weight: 190 Origin: Round 4, 2016 Draft (#107 overall)

YEAR	TEAM	LVL	AGE	W	L	SV	G	GS	IP	H	HR	BB/9	K/9	K	GB%	BABIP
2016	WPT	A-	19	2	2	0	10	10	45^2	44	2	2.2	6.1	31	58%	.303
2017	LWD	A	20	5	1	0	13	13	76^2	61	2	2.5	9.3	79	60%	.299
2017	CLR	A+	20	5	2	0	10	10	52^1	43	2	2.6	8.4	49	52%	.289
2018	REA	AA	21	7	6	0	18	18	106^2	97	13	3.5	8.4	100	53%	.286
2019	PHI	MLB	22	1	1	0	3	3	15	14	2	3.3	8.4	14	48%	.294

Breakout: 13% Improve: 18% Collapse: 12% Attrition: 22% MLB: 38%
Comparables: Scott Barnes, Keyvius Sampson, Jarred Cosart

Sometimes, less is more. In Romero's case, shortening and simplifying his arsenal made a huge difference. From May 9 until a season-ending oblique injury in late July, Romero averaged more than six innings per start and held hitters to a .604 OPS, thanks in large part to an early emphasis on fastball-cutter attacks the first time through, followed by an introduction of changeups into the mix. Romero's run from May through July was good enough to earn him Player of the Year honors for the Reading Fightin' Phils and, thankfully, his injury isn't expected to linger into 2019. It wouldn't be unreasonable to see Romero start this season repeating Double-A, nor would it be a shock to see him quickly promoted if his new approach still proves effective.

YEAR	TEAM	LVL	AGE	WHIP	ERA	DRA	WARP	MPH	FB%	WHF	CSP
2016	WPT	A-	19	1.20	2.56	3.64	0.9				
2017	LWD	A	20	1.07	2.11	2.95	2.1				
2017	CLR	A+	20	1.11	2.24	3.28	1.2				
2018	REA	AA	21	1.29	3.80	4.61	0.9				
2019	PHI	MLB	22	1.28	4.17	4.39	0.1				

LINEOUTS

Hitters

HITTER	POS	TEAM	LVL	AGE	PA	R	2B	3B	HR	RBI	BB	K	SB	CS	AVG/OBP/SLG	DRC+	WARP
Lane Adams	CF	IOW	AAA	28	98	8	2	1	0	6	13	32	9	3	.136/.265/.185	37	-0.8
	CF	GWN	AAA	28	101	9	5	1	0	6	5	37	3	1	.191/.238/.266	34	-0.6
	CF	ATL	MLB	28	29	10	1	0	2	6	4	8	1	0	.240/.345/.520	84	0.2
Daniel Brito	2B	LWD	A	20	368	33	13	2	4	31	27	64	15	6	.252/.309/.340	86	0.2
	2B	CLR	A+	20	100	8	5	2	0	7	6	19	1	1	.250/.300/.348	74	-0.1
Dylan Cozens	RF	LEH	AAA	24	348	49	17	2	21	58	46	124	9	6	.246/.345/.529	126	1.4
	RF	PHI	MLB	24	44	2	2	0	1	2	6	24	1	0	.158/.273/.289	40	-0.3
Arquimedes Gamboa	SS	CLR	A+	20	497	49	14	4	2	37	53	111	6	4	.214/.304/.279	74	-0.6
Deivi Grullon	C	REA	AA	22	353	36	14	1	21	59	18	81	0	0	.273/.310/.515	106	-1.0
Rafael Marchan	C	WPT	A-	19	210	28	8	2	0	12	11	18	9	6	.301/.343/.362	135	1.2
Simon Muzziotti	CF	LWD	A	19	299	33	12	2	1	20	14	40	18	4	.263/.299/.331	84	0.5
Gift Ngoepe	3B	TOR	MLB	28	19	2	0	0	0	0	1	12	0	0	.056/.105/.056	50	-0.1
	3B	BUF	AAA	28	159	15	3	1	2	8	25	63	2	1	.168/.304/.252	65	0.2
Jhailyn Ortiz	RF	LWD	A	19	454	51	18	2	13	47	35	148	2	2	.225/.297/.375	87	-0.8
Gregorio Petit	UT	ROC	AAA	33	312	31	12	1	1	29	17	47	4	1	.268/.313/.327	89	0.8
	UT	MIN	MLB	33	67	7	2	0	0	3	6	14	3	1	.246/.313/.279	81	0.2
Trevor Plouffe	INF	PHI	MLB	32	12	1	0	0	1	3	0	6	0	0	.250/.250/.500	76	0.0
	INF	LEH	AAA	32	274	31	16	0	12	37	41	68	2	0	.230/.347/.460	127	0.9
Cornelius Randolph	LF	REA	AA	21	465	52	18	0	5	40	48	92	3	3	.241/.324/.322	81	-1.0
Sean Rodriguez	2B	IND	AAA	33	42	5	0	1	2	7	5	10	1	1	.250/.357/.444	124	0.3
	2B	PIT	MLB	33	173	21	5	1	5	19	22	60	1	0	.167/.277/.313	65	0.0
Andrew Romine	SS	SEA	MLB	32	131	15	2	1	0	2	7	39	1	0	.210/.260/.244	58	-0.1
Mitch Walding	3B	LEH	AAA	25	472	70	20	2	19	69	73	148	2	0	.265/.390/.474	137	3.7
	3B	PHI	MLB	25	19	1	0	0	1	2	2	12	0	0	.059/.158/.235	53	-0.1

Besides having a solid Twitter account and the ability to play all three outfield spots in a pinch, **Lane Adams** displays impressive business skills by offering advertising for your company in place of his walk-up music. ⓥ **Daniel Brito** has seemingly slipped from "sleeper" back to "pipe dream," as his offensive abilities have yet to overcome the challenges of post-rookie league ball. ⓥ If he's going to help reprise the Double-A Reading "Bash Brothers" tandem he and Hoskins formed in 2016, **Dylan Cozens** will need to find a way to put the bat on the ball more often. ⓥ Still raw in nearly every sense of the word, **Arquimedes Gamboa**'s most likely future is one of a defensive super-sub, with any shred of offensive value simply considered a bonus. ⓥ **Deivi Grullon** really likes to swing, and his career-doubling 21 home runs can only reinforce that particular habit. ⓥ **Rafael Marchan** has yet to homer as a pro, but has a strong throwing arm and struck out just 18 times in 210 plate appearances in his first season stateside. Is it too soon to start hunting for the next Willians Astudillo? (Yes.) ⓥ Out with

Carlos Tocci, in with **Simon Muzziotti** as the torch-bearer for athletic Phillies minor league center fielders in need of some beefier arms. ⓧ There's nothing wrong with a glove-first player until he becomes a glove-only player. When **Gift Ngoepe**'s bat once again failed to materialize alongside his magnetic defense, the Blue Jays signed, sealed and delivered him to the Sydney Blue Sox of the Australian Baseball League. ⓧ **Jhailyn Ortiz** ranked ahead of Vladimir Guerrero, Jr., in the 2015 international class, which just seems cruel at this point. The athleticism remains, though at the moment it's most evident on empty follow-throughs. ⓧ **Gregorio Petit** has played in the majors for parts of six seasons, spread over 11 years, because general managers sometimes pick their utility infielders using random number generators. ⓧ **Trevor Plouffe**'s 16th-inning walk-off home run in late July proved that Enrique Hernandez can't actually play *every* position well. ⓧ Another even year, another hundred-point OPS drop from the previous season for **Cornelius Randolph**, who could only muster 23 extra-base hits with a full season of FirstEnergy Stadium as his home park in 2018. ⓧ Seventy days after "**Sean Rodriguez** Bobblehead Day" at PNC Park, the Pirates granted Rodriguez his unconditional release. The Pirates did not commemorate a bobblehead to mark the occasion. ⓧ The Mariners let **Andrew Romine** spend all of 2018 on the big league roster. As he was both very bad at baseball and exceedingly quiet, we can only assume he positioned himself behind Nelson Cruz whenever the team's executives were around, and they forgot he was there. You can always tell a Romine Man. ⓧ **Mitch Walding** eventually delivered a home run for his first career hit after 14 empty trips to start his career. Did it come against a position player pitching? Sure. Was it still a real Major League homer that counted for two actual runs? You bet!

Pitchers

PITCHER	TEAM	LVL	AGE	W	L	SV	G	GS	IP	H	HR	BB/9	K/9	K	GB%	WHIP	ERA	DRA	WARP
Drew Anderson	LEH	AAA	24	9	4	0	19	19	104^2	92	14	2.5	7.2	84	37%	1.16	3.87	4.13	1.7
	PHI	MLB	24	0	1	0	5	1	12^2	17	0	1.4	7.8	11	43%	1.50	4.97	4.85	0.0
Kyle Dohy	LWD	A	21	3	3	7	24	0	33^2	16	1	4.5	16.8	63	46%	0.98	0.80	1.56	1.3
	CLR	A+	21	2	1	2	7	0	11	5	1	2.5	14.7	18	42%	0.73	1.64	1.21	0.5
	REA	AA	21	2	5	1	18	0	22^2	13	3	8.7	11.9	30	37%	1.54	5.56	4.80	0.0
Bailey Falter	CLR	A+	21	8	4	0	17	17	93^2	87	6	1.4	8.0	83	50%	1.09	2.69	4.66	0.7
Spencer Howard	LWD	A	21	9	8	0	23	23	112	101	6	3.2	11.8	147	40%	1.26	3.78	3.46	2.3
Mauricio Llovera	CLR	A+	22	8	7	0	23	22	121	100	14	2.5	10.2	137	42%	1.11	3.72	3.43	2.7
Francisco Morales	WPT	A-	18	4	5	0	13	13	56^1	54	6	5.3	10.9	68	42%	1.54	5.27	3.82	0.9
David Parkinson	LWD	A	22	8	1	0	17	17	95^1	74	4	2.5	10.9	115	46%	1.05	1.51	3.04	2.4
	CLR	A+	22	3	0	0	5	4	29	17	1	2.8	8.1	26	42%	0.90	1.24	3.85	0.5
Ramon Rosso	LWD	A	22	5	1	0	12	12	67^2	45	3	2.7	10.8	81	51%	0.96	1.33	3.29	1.5
	CLR	A+	22	6	2	0	11	10	55^2	49	1	3.2	9.4	58	50%	1.24	2.91	3.65	1.1
Connor Seabold	CLR	A+	22	4	4	0	12	12	71^2	57	6	1.8	8.5	68	47%	0.99	3.77	3.31	1.7
	REA	AA	22	1	4	0	11	11	58^2	55	10	2.9	9.8	64	36%	1.26	4.91	3.46	1.3
Kyle Young	LWD	A	20	3	3	0	9	9	52^1	46	2	1.2	7.6	44	64%	1.01	3.10	2.90	1.4

Drew Anderson neither improved nor worsened his outlook as a potential depth option in the rotation or the bullpen. That we're saying this about the last pick of the 21st round of the 2012 draft means Anderson is already a success, no matter the ultimate outcome. ⚾ Striking out 81 of 172 batters is a performance that will raise eyebrows in any organization, and **Kyle Dohy** deserved a quick promotion with those eye-popping numbers. Alas, walking 22 of 101 hitters in Double-A only managed to raise a single eyebrow. ⚾ Considered a project when the Phillies took him in the fifth round, **Bailey Falter** has instead moved quickly. The concern is that he's aging straight into a fifth starter before his time, unless he can find some heat or an out pitch. ⚾ 2017 2nd-round pick **Spencer Howard** struck out 67 of the last 190 batters he faced in 2018, and capped off the year with a postseason no-hitter. The fastball and slider are sharp, so there's floor for days here. ⚾ In English, *Llovera* means "will rain." As far as **Mauricio Llovera** is concerned, the Phillies certainly hope he keeps making his mid-90s heat and those low-80s curves rain down for Ks. ⚾ 2016 J2 pickup **Francisco Morales**, only just turned 19, is already touching mid-90s with his fastball. His is a name to remember and forget and remember three or four more times in the coming years. ⚾ Over his first 157 professional innings, **David Parkinson** has a 1.55 ERA with a K/BB ratio over 4, and has only given up 7 homers. Greater tests of validity await him in Double-A, but it's hard not to be impressed with this start.

Philadelphia Phillies 2019

Ⓧ **Ramon Rosso** has been a little old for each level he's played at in two pro seasons, but at least he's making use of his advantage, via a 1.76 ERA and 244 strikeouts in 199 innings. Ⓧ With flowing locks and a high leg kick from the right side, you'd be forgiven mistaking **Connor Seabold** for Bronson Arroyo. When the ball jumps upward off the bat, you'd be equally forgiven then, too. Ⓧ If **Kyle Young** were any taller, he'd probably be able to reach the catcher's mitt from the mound, which would result in a pretty interesting morality experiment for hitters swinging at a ball still in a pitcher's hand as it crossed the plate.

Phillies Prospects

The State of the System:
The system has thinned out significantly through graduations, but the Phillies are ready to contend and still have a fair bit of pitching depth at least.

The Top Ten:

1 Sixto Sanchez   RHP   OFP: 70   Likely: 55
ETA: Mid-to-late 2019, pending his availability to pitch.
Born: 07/29/98   Age: 20   Bats: R   Throws: R   Height: 6'0"   Weight: 185
Origin: International Free Agent, 2015

The Report: The official pitching prospect of the BP Prospect Team finally ran into some trouble, but it wasn't on the mound, it was in the doctor's office. Sanchez was chugging right along on his path of destruction when he came down with elbow soreness in early June, and he never returned to game action. He was throwing in fall instructs, and the word around town was that he was just as impressive as always. The Phillies scheduled his comeback for the Arizona Fall League… and then scratched him with collarbone soreness just before that league started.

When healthy, he regularly blasts it into the triple-digits and throws a kitchen sink of pitches that flash above-average to plus-plus. At various points we've seen a four-seamer, a sinker, a cutter, a slider, a slow curve, another breaking ball in between that you could call a slurve, a regular change with circle-type action, and a harder change that moves like a split-change, and they're *all* good. Whether or not these are distinct pitches or flavors and manipulations on a core four-pitch arsenal is sort of irrelevant. We expect him to pick four or five eventually, and he could settle in with a monster repertoire.

Sanchez has frequently been so dominant on the mound as to appear like he isn't being challenged. He will often spend an inning or two, and sometimes even a whole game, working on refining a core offering, as we've also seen from past higher-end Phillies pitching prospects. He's good enough to do this and still pitch effectively, but it does make evaluating his overall deception and sequencing tougher than we'd like. He's also clearly much shorter than listed, which does raise the usual short guy issues like durability and fastball plane.

The Risks: We've heard his name and "potential Tommy John surgery" mentioned far too often together to call it low risk, and we've lowered the likely grade by a half-tick to account for the chance that he can't handle a starting workload. The profile itself is low-to-medium risk. The stuff and command are already there for a fine MLB pitcher, with ace potential, and he might've made the majors in 2018 if healthy.

Ben Carsley's Fantasy Take: It doesn't take a genius to see that the number of 200-plus IP workhorse aces is likely to decrease in the next few years. The few among that class who remain are insanely valuable, yes, but there's also plenty of value to be found in a guy like Sanchez, who may strike out more dudes in 160 innings than, let's say Rick Porcello will in 200. Even if you want to factor in an 18-month layoff at some point for what feels like (but is not actually) the inevitable Tommy John surgery and recovery, Sanchez should be dominating MLB lineups by late 2020 at the latest. He's still a top-three fantasy starting pitching prospect, and he's gonna be insanely fun to watch.

2. Adonis Medina   RHP   OFP: 60   Likely: 50
ETA: Probably 2020, but 2019 is in play
Born: 12/18/96   Age: 22   Bats: R   Throws: R   Height: 6'1"   Weight: 185
Origin: International Free Agent, 2014

The Report: Unlike Sanchez, Medina mostly just kept chugging along in 2018. There wasn't a big step forward, like he had with velocity or the slider in 2017, but there wasn't a big step back or a concerning injury either. He's still pretty consistently in the 91-96 velocity band and he still scrapes a little higher. He still has a smooth, athletic delivery and an advanced feel for pitching. Depending on your descriptive preferences, he's either dropped his so-so loopy curve for a slider, or tightened the curve into a harder slurve. It's semantics, and the important part is that he has a low-80s breaking ball with slidery movement (and we've usually called it a slider) that looks above-average already and projects to get to plus or better. The cambio remains inconsistent.

He didn't put up an overwhelming topline in the Florida State League, although his 2018 strikeout/walk rates are similar to his 2017. The rise in Medina's runs allowed numbers are basically all due to five games where he gave up five or more runs and didn't make it out of the third inning. We'll flag consistency as something to watch for in the future; for now this might just be a quirky statistical oddity.

Medina's stock is pretty much steady from last year, but he's risen three spots on this list. Suffice to say, this system has seen a lot of attrition from graduations, trades, and slowly-developing draft picks recently.

The Risks: Medium. He's going to need a better third pitch to stay in the rotation. He could use more consistent command, while we're at it. We need to see him get high-minors batters out. These are pretty typical risks for a good A-ball pitching prospect, honestly.

Ben Carsley's Fantasy Take: Medina is among my favorite prospects with this fairly standard profile. In general we favor upside over probability, but Medina is close enough to the majors and has just high enough of a ceiling now to probably warrant top-101 inclusion. He won't win you leagues, but he might be your fantasy SP5 for several years. You could do worse!

3

Spencer Howard   RHP   OFP: 60   Likely: 50   ETA: 2021
Born: 07/28/96   Age: 22   Bats: R   Throws: R   Height: 6'3"   Weight: 205
Origin: Round 2, 2017 Draft (#45 overall)

The Report: Remember all of that stuff I just wrote about Adonis Medina? Welcome to part two of the report. Howard sits a free and easy 92-96 with the fastball and regularly touches a tick or two higher, and we've gotten reliable though occasional reports of triple-digits. He blew through the South Atlantic League in a manner that looked a lot like Medina's 2017 campaign. Howard throws the four-pitch starter mix, and there's an above-average slider here along with a useful changeup and curveball. He's a big, durable-looking guy, and just watching him on the mound, you wouldn't expect him to have trouble handling a starter's workload.

Howard ranks below Medina because he's around a year-and-a-half behind on the development curve—Howard's five months older and a level lower, and he only made 14 starts in college before signing as a draft-eligible sophomore. Even considering that, it's still a bit odd that the Phillies left him in Lakewood all season.

The Risks: Medium, and again pretty similar to Medina's. Due to limited experience as a starting pitcher for his age, there's sneaky reliever risk here for a guy with no obvious health, injury, or pitch deficiencies. Then again, is it strictly speaking "risk" if the fastball/slider combo plays up there?

Ben Carsley's Fantasy Take: Maybe I'm just not as up on my Phillies pitching prospects as the rest of my dynasty-playing compatriots, but I was surprised to see such a positive report on Howard. He may not have flashy upside, but I believe he's being pretty undervalued right now if his fantasy comparison is "Medina from a year ago." Players like this often go overlooked in drafts held primarily for new entrants into the dynasty pool. But if you're in round 3 or 4 of one such draft this year and see no inspiring options, maybe check to see if Howard is owned instead.

4. Alec Bohm 3B

OFP: 60 Likely: 50 ETA: Late 2020
Born: 08/03/96 Age: 22 Bats: R Throws: R Height: 6'5" Weight: 225
Origin: Round 1, 2018 Draft (#3 overall)

The Report: Bohm was a premium college performer at Wichita State with the best combination of hit and raw power in his draft class. He has a wood bat track record from the Cape in 2017 and was the third overall pick in the draft. He should be higher than this, right? People are going to think we have a vendetta against every Phillies first round pick at this rate.

So, the problems: Bohm is a great hitter but often prioritizes contact and shortness to the ball over fully tapping into his 7 raw. He struggled in his first professional summer—with the reports to match—although his time in short-season was marred by minor injuries. The long-term concern is his ultimate defensive home. It's not a bad body, but it's a big one, and he isn't rangy at the hot corner. Bohm has plenty of arm for the left side, although he can struggle with his accuracy at times. This whole profile could go R/R first base at some point, which means that pop will have to become a priority. We'd also like to see him settle in during 2019 and really mash too.

The Risks: Medium, which I suppose is higher than you'd like for a top-five college bat. He may end up a hit over power third baseman who isn't a great defender there. He also might end up the best overall hitter in his draft class if it all comes together.

Ben Carsley's Fantasy Take: Bohm is pretty clearly the second-best fantasy prospect in this system and one of the better new bats in the dynasty pool. The defensive concerns aren't as pressing for us—he just needs to stay 3B eligible rather than play there every day—and he's got a decent timeline to fantasy relevancy as a college bat. In our midseason top 50 dynasty prospects lists, Bohm slotted in at No. 30 and we compared his upside to Good Eugenio Suarez. That still tracks.

5. Luis Garcia SS

OFP: 60 Likely: 50 ETA: 2023
Born: 10/01/00 Age: 18 Bats: B Throws: R Height: 5'11" Weight: 170
Origin: International Free Agent, 2017

The Report: Not that Luis Garcia of the Phillies, or that Luis Garcia the shortstop prospect, but he's arguably the best of the Luises Garcia. He's got sure-shot shortstop tools with plus range and arm strength. It's a smaller frame with some projection left but he should maintain his athleticism at 22. Garcia has good barrel control, but lacks physicality and loft in the swing, so power's never going to be a big part of this profile. So we can feel very confident about the glove, and see what the hit tool looks like at… well, 22. If it is a plus hit tool, the Phillies could have a top-of-the-order tablesetter and a Wilson Pickit at the 6. If it doesn't, the glove and speed could still propel Garcia to the majors in a complementary role.

The Risks: Can I use very high? Obviously he is a 17-year-old shortstop in the complex, but the combo of glove and hit seems like it keeps him below extreme.

Ben Carsley's Fantasy Take: Let this serve as proof that I'm not unreasonably high on *every* shortstop prospect named Luis Garcia. That being said, I like the Phillies' version plenty too, and he could be a very fast dynasty riser. Honestly, he's exactly the type of guy Bret and I often put in the back of the top-101 as a flier, and only his ETA (and to a certain extent the lack of pop) keeps him from making the list with ease.

6

Adam Haseley   OF OFP: 55   Likely: 45   ETA: Late-2019/early-2020
Born: 04/12/96   Age: 23   Bats: L   Throws: L   Height: 6'1"   Weight: 195
Origin: Round 1, 2017 Draft (#8 overall)

The Report: Hitters gonna hit. Haseley was drafted based on his advanced hit tool, and he hit .300 in his first full season and made it to Double-A. We're still concerned about how the overall profile plays, because the secondary skills past said hit tool and his arm (he was an early-round prospect as a pitcher too) get worrisome. His future defensive home in the outfield isn't clear, and it would help his stock a lot if he could settle into center field. The power projection is still only fringe-average to average. There's a lot less "wow" here than you'd hope for given his draft position, but he puts the bat on the ball with authority often enough that you can reasonably hope that the hit tool carries it all.

Haseley's 2018 performance feels better than it was because of that shiny .300 marker—if you drop him to .295 at Clearwater it doesn't actually matter, but it would feel like he's a much worse prospect. An ACC batting champion popped in the top ten for his advanced bat and hit tool should hit .300 in A-ball. The Double-A performance is encouraging, and we're a little more optimistic than we were last year. That said, as we have to note every year, Reading is one of the biggest launching pads east of the Rockies.

The Risks: Medium. He might tweener out, and he's already played a lot of corner outfield. We're concerned about the lack of game power. If he's more of a .270 hitter than a .300 hitter, the profile gets tough. He might end up being really duplicative of Nick Williams, and the Phillies might just go sign Bryce Harper to play over both anyway.

Ben Carsley's Fantasy Take: The hope here is that Haseley is able to routinely do something similar to what Corey Dickerson did in 2018: hit .300 with ~15 homers, a handful of steals and respectable RBI/R totals. That well-rounded approach was good enough to help Dickerson be a top-40 outfielder in 5x5 leagues, per ESPN. The problem is that if Haseley comes up short in even one or two of those cats, you're looking at more of a back fantasy OF option in the vein of 2018 Gerardo Parra (.284 with 6 homers and 11 steals, no. 60 OF). That doesn't make him a *bad* fantasy prospect per se, just one who's overvalued based on his draft pedigree.

7. Enyel De Los Santos   RHP

OFP: 55   Likely: 45   ETA: Debuted in 2018
Born: 12/25/95   Age: 23   Bats: R   Throws: R   Height: 6'3"   Weight: 170
Origin: International Free Agent, 2014

The Report: De Los Santos has been a bit lost in the shuffle in the Padres and Phillies systems the last two years. You'd think a mid-90s power sinker would garner would more attention, but given the sheer breadth of good pitching prospects his two orgs have had, it takes more than that. His breaking balls bleed together a bit. The slider he's added doesn't always tease out from his curve which is still the more advanced breaker despite being a bit of a short 12-6. Either or both can get slurvy. Both have a chance to be average or a tick above. Neither gets used as much as his advanced change. It can be a bit firm at times and act more like a two-seam fastball, but it will also flash above-average fade. De Los Santos has an ideal frame and a compact arm action and has always thrown strikes, save for his 2018 MLB cameo. Ultimately though, he may lack a true swing-and-miss offering to be more than a backend starter.

The Risks: Low. He might end up a reliever. He might only be the sixth best starter on the 2019 Phillies, but he's close to a finished product.

Ben Carsley's Fantasy Take: It's not just that De Los Santos may not start long-term; it's that even if he does, he's not likely to miss as many bats as you'd need him to. He might be perma-rosterable in his prime or if he ends up in a better home ballpark, but right now he looks like a fantasy spot starter.

8. Mickey Moniak   OF

OFP: 55   Likely: 40   ETA: 2022
Born: 05/13/98   Age: 21   Bats: L   Throws: R   Height: 6'2"   Weight: 185
Origin: Round 1, 2016 Draft (#1 overall)

The Report: Well, it went better than 2017 at least, as Moniak was almost a league-average hitter in the Florida State League. But at the same time, we ranked him last year with some expectation that there could be a big rebound to something closer to his draft status, and instead he's settled in as a medium-upside, high-variance type.

The party piece was supposed to be a plus or plus-plus hit tool, and it just hasn't shown up in pro ball. I think the ultimate underlying force here is an inability to recognize spin, which in turn leads to weak, defensive contact and bad swing habits across the board. That's not entirely unchangeable, and the higher-end bat control is still there, which is why he's sometimes managed league average performance. He's more likely than Haseley to stay in center, and he's a good athlete overall.

We're contractually obligated by Phillies Twitter to tell you that over 2018's last 49 games, Moniak hit .312/.365/.487—the type of performance we envisioned when he was drafted. But the 150 games before the last 49 matter too, and he was dreadfully bad in those. If there's a major change lurking underneath, it hasn't evidenced itself yet, and a hot six weeks on its own is no more important this time than when he had a similar run early in 2017.

The Risks: High. "He might not actually be good at baseball" is a pretty big risk. Expectations remain tremendously and unfairly high on him as a former first-overall pick. He's a prospect, he's just a decent one with a lot of questions instead of a high-probability impact player. It's not what you want from 1.1.

Ben Carsley's Fantasy Take: If you roster 200-plus prospects like in a TDGX-sized format, you're stuck with Moniak unless someone hasn't read the baseball news in two years. You might as well hold on and see if he at least develops into an OF5, or if you can flip him if he has another six-week hot streak. If your league only rosters 100-or-so prospects, he's safe to drop and has been for a while. It's a bummer, but best not to cling to past hopes.

9. JoJo Romero   LHP   OFP: 50   Likely: 45
ETA: 2019 in spot duty, 2020 in force
Born: 09/09/96   Age: 22   Bats: L   Throws: L   Height: 6'0"   Weight: 190
Origin: Round 4, 2016 Draft (#107 overall)

The Report: Romero just happens to be sandwiched between the highest variance prospects in the system, but he's a pretty stable commodity himself. He's a fairly standard three-pitch, short, good-command lefty prospect, with all of the positives and negatives that implies.

Romero sits in the high-80s to low-90s with the fastball, although it'll pop higher occasionally. He'll often show an above-average slider and an average changeup, and every now and then you'll get a fourth pitch, a show-me curve. He has very good command and pitchability. He's not ranked aggressively here because he might not have an out pitch, and he's on the short side.

Romero pitched well for much of the season as a 21-year-old in Double-A before going down in mid-July to an oblique injury. It's not sexy and Ben Carsley is about to tell you how these guys don't win you fantasy leagues, but he has the makings of an MLB contributor, and he's on the doorstep of the majors.

The Risks: Low. Romero may not have great upside, but he's as good of a bet as anyone outside of the top two for a significant MLB career.

Ben Carsley's Fantasy Take: Whether you should have any interest in Romero depends entirely on your league size and setup. Deep leagues where average-ish innings eaters count for something? Draft away. Shallow leagues or circuits with innings caps where performance matters more than bulk innings? For sure not.

10. Jhailyn Ortiz   OF   OFP: 50   Likely: 40   ETA: 2023
Born: 11/18/98   Age: 20   Bats: R   Throws: R   Height: 6'3"   Weight: 215
Origin: International Free Agent, 2015

The Report: Huge dude, huge swing, huge swing-and-miss. We were setting everything up to be on the Ortiz hype train this season, but he fell flat on his face in his full-season debut at Lakewood.

Ortiz shows off plus-plus raw power and extreme bat speed. He also has a long, long swing and gets beat with velocity in the zone and by chasing outside it. He didn't show much barrel control or ability to adjust to full-season pitching, but it's early and he'd shown better on these things previously. A spring shoulder injury provides something of an excuse, and given his powerful stroke and bonus size, he's going to get plenty of chances.

He's athletic for his size, but his size is also enormous (no matter what they're claiming in the program). It's easy to envision a future where he's limited to first base or even DH, and at that point his reasonable upside starts to resemble C.J. Cron. That kind of bat looks a lot better in right field.

The Risks: Extreme. It's not a similar body to Jose Pujols, but it's sort of a similar skill set. If Ortiz gets it together he could be high up the 101 in a year or two's time; he could also stall out in A-ball.

Ben Carsley's Fantasy Take: Sorry, I went into a coma after "the reasonable upside starts to look like C.J. Cron."

The Next Five:

11 Arquimedes Gamboa SS
Born: 09/23/97   Age: 21   Bats: B   Throws: R   Height: 6'0"   Weight: 175
Origin: International Free Agent, 2014

This is why you have to be a bit cautious about Mickey Moniak's big late-season surge. Gamboa was unconscious towards the end of 2017 in Lakewood, driving the ball with authority and looking for all the world like he was breaking out. He even had a narrative explanation in that he finally recovered from a hamstring injury that bothered him for much of the season. Then he went to the Florida State League and his slugging percentage started with a 2; it didn't get much better in the AFL.

The Phillies protected Gamboa from the Rule 5 Draft despite a crowded farm, because he can go get it at shortstop already and would've made an obvious selection for a tanking team. In doing so, they started the clock on how long he has to get his offensive game together. It's a catch-22.

12 Ranger Suarez LHP
Born: 08/26/95   Age: 23   Bats: L   Throws: L   Height: 6'1"   Weight: 180
Origin: International Free Agent, 2012

See JoJo Romero. Adjust quality of slider down. Stir in warm water. Rinse. Repeat.

Suarez is pretty similar to Romero overall, except he's more balanced between the slider and changeup and has even less upside. He also made the majors faster—40-man considerations sometimes matter here—although he didn't pitch well in spot start duty. The Phillies don't seem particularly interested in handing him a spot on the staff, so he's probably headed to Triple-A to try to consolidate things and wait for an opportunity to fill in.

13 Francisco Morales   RHP
Born: 10/27/99   Age: 19   Bats: R   Throws: R   Height: 6'4"   Weight: 185
Origin: International Free Agent, 2016

The Phillies have had a lot of luck with five-figure bonus arms in Latin America in recent years. Morales was their first seven-figure one in a while and early returns have been mostly good. He has an athletic, uptempo delivery and will flash mid-90s heat at times. This will vary start-to-start and within starts as well. Sometimes it will be more low-90s and he can dip into the 80s at times too. The slider is potentially plus, a tight two-plane breaker that has more present polish and command than you'd expect in an 18-year-old short-season arm. Morales needs more consistency with the velocity and an actual third pitch at some point, but the upside here is as high as any of the arms in the back half of the top ten.

14 Rafael Marchan   C
Born: 02/25/99   Age: 20   Bats: B   Throws: R   Height: 5'9"   Weight: 170
Origin: International Free Agent, 2015

And here come the catchers! You can have worse player development strategies than to collect as many viable backstops as possible, because, well, catchers are weird. Marchan got $200k from the Phillies. He played some shortstop as an amateur but is very much built like a catcher. He's new to the position and will be a project behind the plate, but he has the raw physical tools to be a solid catcher in time. Marchan has already shown extremely impressive bat-to-ball skills for his age and level, so he may be more a bat-first backstop in the end, unlike…

15 Rodolfo Duran   C
Born: 02/19/98   Age: 21   Bats: R   Throws: R   Height: 5'9"   Weight: 181
Origin: International Free Agent, 2015

Catchers remain weird. Duran wasn't hugely on the radar coming into the season, and started off sharing time with organizational soldier Gregori Rivero. Very quickly, it became clear that Duran was actually an interesting prospect. He's a short, stout man who looks like a catcher, and he takes a big uppercut out of an open stance. It works for him because there's a lot of power here. He's also potentially a dude behind the plate, with a strong arm and the early signs of decent hands. What isn't there yet is his hit tool—contact is a real problem and he could get eaten alive at higher levels—but a 20-year-old catcher who projects for power and defense is a real prospect.

Others of note:

Deivi Grullon, C, Double-A Reading

The raw power we've long trumpeted showed up in games this year for Grullon—but how much did playing in Reading help? He hit much better overall within the friendly confines of FirstEnergy than he did in the rest of the Eastern League, with 14 of his 21 dingers at home. Grullon has always flashed a lot of arm strength, and he has a simple swing that can make the ball go a long way. Pitch selectivity remains a problem, however, and limits his hit tool. The Phillies left him off the 40-man roster, and catchers who can be MLB backups now but have some upside are Rule 5 staples; there were no takers.

Daniel Brito, 2B, Low-A Lakewood

Brito was also left off the 40-man and exposed to the Rule 5 draft, but he's in no way ready. We've spilled a lot of ink on Brito here at Baseball Prospectus, so let's summarize where he's at now: He's a fine defender at second who has rarely tapped into his above-average raw power, hasn't taken advantage of the sweet lefty swing that makes you think he should have a plus hit tool, and is prone to lapses on the field. He's only 20, he hasn't been that bad in A-ball, he's still quite athletic, and will often do something to keep you believing. He was one of the better prospects available in the last Rule 5 Draft, but like Pedro Gonzalez from Texas, he'd be nearly impossible to keep on a competitive roster.

Mauricio Llovera, RHP, Complex-Level GCL

I'll be honest and say that I didn't really see Mauricio Llovera as a guy entering this season. He yo-yo'd between the rotation and the pen in Lakewood in 2017, and he seemed like every 95-and-a-slider short middle relief prospect you see a half-dozen times in any given series now. Then he went out and threw 121 good innings in the Clearwater rotation with reports of an improved changeup and far greater consistency. The build and recoil still point toward a future relief role, and I'd like to see him pull the act off again in Double-A before I jump in with both feet. But there's more here than I thought at first glance.

Kyle Dohy, LHP, High-A Clearwater

You can find them everywhere now. Kyle Dohy was a 16th round pick in 2017 who was a terrible college starter and a terrible short-season reliever after the draft. Then he spent last offseason working with agent-slash-pitching guru-slash-former prospect Caleb Cotham, completely reworking his mechanics and arsenal using advanced video and training technologies. He emerged as a lefty shoving in the mid-90s with an untouchable slider, and he sliced and diced his way to Double-A by mid-July. He ran into some walk problems up there while trying to reintroduce his changeup, but over the course of the season he pushed his way from non-prospect to the cusp of the majors.

Top Talents 25 and Under (born 4/1/93 or later):

1. Aaron Nola
2. Sixto Sanchez
3. Jorge Alfaro
4. Nick Williams
5. Seranthony Dominguez
6. Adonis Medina
7. Scott Kingery
8. Spencer Howard
9. Alec Bohm
10. Luis Garcia

Aaron Nola is an ace. We no longer need to qualify that. He's just one of the best half-dozen starting pitchers in the game right now. Little more needs to be said here.

The prospect-industrial complex spent much of the past decade arguing about what Jorge Alfaro and Nick Williams would become. Amusingly, they both look like they're settling in as perfectly good regular MLB players—not elite guys, and not busts. Alfaro's defense has developed much more than most predicted, but his bat is only acceptable for the position. Williams was just a touch above a league-average hitter by DRC+, although we have him giving away pretty much all of that value in the field. They are both chugging along on their median projections at the moment.

Seranthony Dominguez entered camp as an oft-injured A-ball pitcher with inconsistent velocity while starting and a breaking ball that flashed; he was the best reliever in the Phillies bullpen by mid-May. He sat 100 or close to it all year, with a devastating low-90s slider and the occasional change at similar velocity. He's never starting again unless it's as part of an opener gambit, but all signs point to a dominant high-leverage reliever into his 30s. If you were ranking the big leaguers just on what they are right now, Dominguez would be at least two spots higher on this list.

Scott Kingery signed by far the biggest contract extension in MLB history for a player with no service time at all before the season, thus eliminating Philadelphia's need to send him down to claw a year back. But Kingery lost all the power he gained in 2017 without any corresponding uptick in contact, leading

Philadelphia Phillies 2019

to a putrid batting line. Maybe he made a good move signing the deal after all. For reasons that never escaped the walls of Citizens Bank Park, the Phillies regularly ran him out at shortstop all year—a position he'd played all of twice in the minors, and one that doesn't suit his defensive talents well. He's still versatile and toolsy, and maybe he'll hit a little more if he's not trying like hell to fight shortstop to a draw.

Some others of note who didn't make it for various reasons: Rhys Hoskins was ineligible by a few weeks, and would've ranked second without much thought for all the reasons you'd think. Zach Eflin was the next-closest to making the list, and would've ranked around or just ahead of Enyel, since you'd take the existing No. 4-type starter over the field of likely No. 4 type starters. Victor Arano was also pretty close, and has an argument if you're more of a believer in the sustainability of his extreme slider-heavy approach. J.P. Crawford likely would've ranked third if he hadn't been dealt for Jean Segura, because I am extremely stubborn.

Part 3: Featured Articles

The Hole in The Shift is Fixing Itself

Russell Carleton

I've been on a bit of a mission against The Shift of late. I'm not out to get The Shift for the usual reasons that people oppose it. The words "the right way to play the game" won't be found on my lips. If a team wants to pursue a strategy that is within the rules and it works, then by all means, they have my blessing (not that they need it). Instead, my concern with The Shift is a worry that it doesn't work, or at least that it has a flaw that needs fixing.

The data show that while The Shift does a decent job of preventing singles on balls in play (what it's supposed to do), it also increases the number of walks that happen in front of it, and the number of additional walks outweighs the number of singles saved. It's a problem because you can't throw a guy out if he gets to walk to first base.

But the "why" was important. It seemed that The Shift was changing the way in which pitchers pitched. We saw that there were fewer fastballs thrown in front of The Shift than we might otherwise expect, and that pitchers tended to stay out of the strike zone a little more. Not by a lot. In fact, it might not even be visible to the naked eye. The percentage of pitches that are out of the zone goes from 51.0 to 53.3 from a standard defense (two right/two left) to a full shift (three on one side). That difference stands up even after we control for the types of hitters that get shifted against. And it's enough to drive up the walk rate to where it cancels out the benefits that teams thought they were getting with The Shift… and then some.

But there was some hope. I found that when individual pitchers stayed closer to the in-zone/out-of-zone mix that they used without The Shift on, they could still get the benefits of The Shift without the walk problems. So, in theory, a team could simply figure out a way to convince its pitchers to not fall prey to the walk trap and The Shift would once again be their friend.

It's reasonable to think that some teams might be more hip to this idea than others. Maybe some figured it out a year before the others. Maybe they were better at getting the message across to their pitchers. Or, maybe no one has figured it out yet.

Warning! Gory Mathematical Details Ahead!

I used data from 2015-2017, made available through MLB's data portal, Baseball Savant. They are kind enough to note when teams are using an infield shift (three fielders on one side of second base), as opposed to a "strategic shift" (someone's playing a bit out of position, but it's not quite that drastic) or a "standard" alignment.

Since we're doing this by team, I can't just look at raw walk rates, because we know that some teams have good pitchers and others have not-so-good pitchers. Some have a mix of both. I used the log-odds ratio method to take into account a batter's general walking proclivities, and a pitcher's as well, and then shoving them into a binary logistic regression. Then, I asked the computer to generate a specific coefficient for each team's pitchers, for when they went into The Shift and how that affected their walk rate.

Using those coefficients, I was able to project what would happen if a league-average pitcher faced a league-average hitter (which we expect would product a league-average walk rate; from 2015-2017, 7.7 percent of plate appearances ended in a walk) and then just switched his hat. Here's the top five and the bottom five:

Top 5 Teams	Projected Shift Walk Rate	Bottom 5 Teams	Projected Shift Walk Rate
Rockies	6.2%	Rangers	11.2%
Pirates	6.7%	Mets	10.4%
Indians	7.2%	Dodgers	10.2%
Astros	7.3%	Cardinals	9.9%
Braves	7.7%	Tigers	9.7%

There are probably people out there right now trying to figure out what the common thread is among the top and bottom teams. I'm sure, because this is Baseball Prospectus, people are already trying to make the case that sabermetric "early adopters" have some sort of edge here. I think that the more interesting piece is that by the time you get to fifth place in The Shift, we're at league average.

As a sanity check, I examined the issue on a pitch-by-pitch level, looking at how often pitchers threw their pitches in the GameDay strike zone, and again using the same basic methodology and getting team-specific coefficients. The names on the list re-arranged themselves, but the idea was the same, and the two lists correlated with an R of .593.

There's a reason that I don't usually do this type of leaderboard post. I don't really know what the Rockies, Pirates, Indians, Astros, and Braves have in common, or what they have that the bottom five don't. I can put a shrug emoji here and say, "Well, it must be something!" but that seems like a cop-out. Instead, I'd like to present another table and suggest that the table above doesn't even really matter anymore.

Year	League Percent Outside K Zone (Full Shift)	League Percent in K Zone (No Shift)	Difference
2015	54.1%	51.1%	3.0%
2016	53.3%	50.9%	2.4%
2017	52.6%	50.9%	1.7%
2018	52.0%	50.7%	1.3%

The hole in The Shift is fixing itself, and it's coming down really fast league wide. In my earlier work on The Shift, I suggested that until teams stopped having such a huge difference between their out-of-zone rate with and without The Shift on, there would just be too many walks for The Shift to make sense. It seems that all 30 of them have been working toward just that. I once estimated that it takes about 10 years for an idea to filter its way through baseball. At this rate, it looks like teams are going to catch up a lot faster than that. And yeah, they're all saber-smart now.

It's likely that whatever magic it was that the Rockies and Pirates had has made its way to Texas and Queens. Or is at least on its way. And if teams are committing to fixing the walk problem, then it's likely that they will continue shifting and shifting a lot.

And eventually it's going to actually make sense for them to do it.

—*Russell Carleton is a former author of Baseball Prospectus and now an analyst for the New York Mets.*

The State of the Quality Start

Rob Mains

One of the seven things you (probably) didn't know about the 2018 season is that quality starts—defined as a start lasting six or more innings with three or fewer earned runs allowed—as a percentage of total starts cratered to an all-time low of 41 percent. I want to look a little more deeply into this, since it's been a while (May of 2016, to be exact) since I've examined quality starts.

The term *quality start* is credited to *Philadelphia Inquirer* sportswriter John Lowe. It's been derided ever since he coined it in December of 1985. Three runs in six innings? That's a 4.50 ERA! In what world is that a measure of quality?

Let's start with that criticism. It's true that 3 x 9 / 6 = 4.5. (You came here for this sort of high-level math, right?) But it's also true that type of start, meeting the bare minimum for earning a quality start, is unusual. Here's the proportion of quality starts in which the pitcher lasted exactly six innings and yielded exactly three earned runs. (I'm going to confine this analysis to the 30-team era, 1998-present. Almost all data retrieved in this article is via the Baseball-Reference Play Index.)

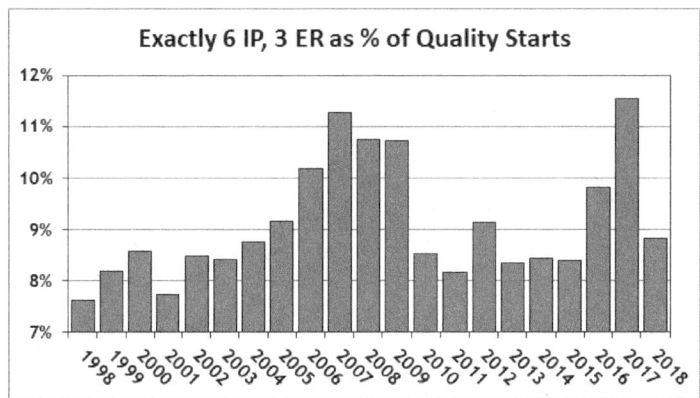

There were 1,997 quality starts in 2018. Only 176, or fewer than one in 11, featured a pitcher going six innings and allowing three earned runs. Put another way, the percentage of quality starts that resulted in a 4.50 ERA (8.8 percent) is less than half the percentage of games in which a batter hit two home runs and his team lost (22.5 percent; 237-69 won-lost). That doesn't impugn hitting two homers.

So if a 4.50 ERA isn't the norm, what is? How good are quality starts?

Pretty good, it turns out. First, on a team level:

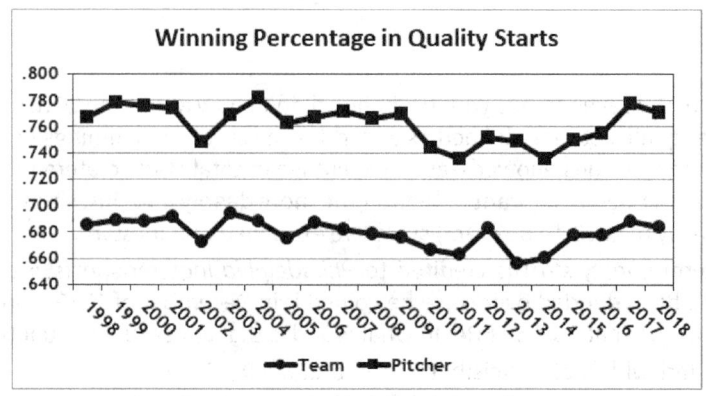

Teams receiving a quality start from their pitcher won 68.4 percent of their games in 2018, in line with the 30-team era average of 67.9 percent. A team with a .684 winning percentage wins 111 games. Getting a quality start is definitely a good thing. Individual pitchers throwing quality starts have a higher winning percentage because a big slice of team losses is assigned to a reliever.

If teams do well in quality starts, how well do the starting pitchers do? Again, very well.

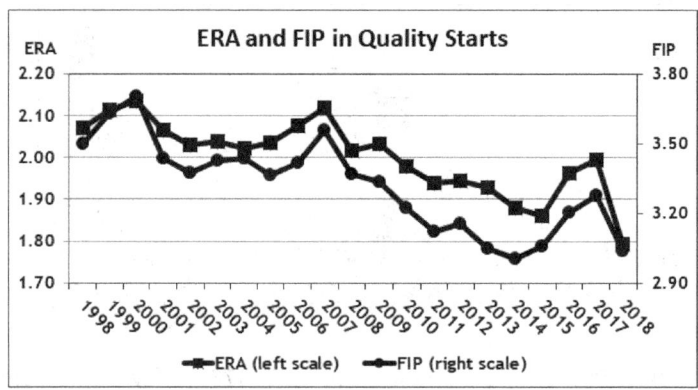

Pitchers in quality starts had a 1.79 ERA (blue line) in 2018, *the lowest in the 30-team era*. Their FIP was higher, 3.04, but still excellent. In the 30-team era, only 2014 had a lower FIP for quality starts, 3.01.

But, of course, the run environment in 2014 was different. Teams in 2014 scored 4.07 runs per game, the fewest in a non-strike year since 1976. They scored 4.45 runs per game in 2018. So surrendering a 3.04 FIP in 2018 is more impressive than 3.01 in 2014. Accordingly, let's look at ERA and FIP in quality starts relative to league averages.

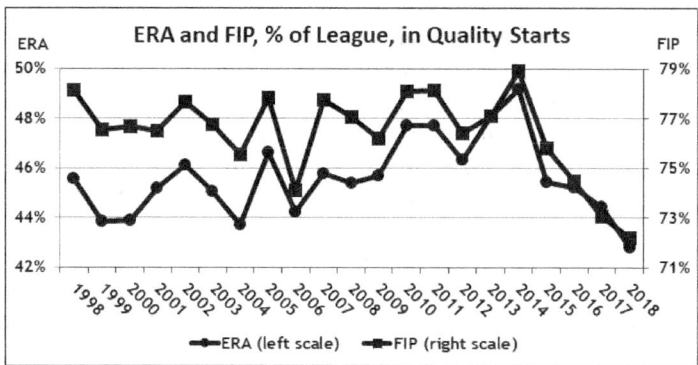

This tells a more dramatic story. Starting pitchers in 2018 gave up a 4.19 ERA and a 4.21 FIP. Starters in quality starts gave up a 1.79 ERA, 43 percent of the league average. Starters in quality starts gave up a 3.04 FIP, 72 percent of the league average. Both of these marks represent lows in the 30-team era.

The takeaway here is this: *Quality starts are better, relative to other starts, than they've ever been over the past 21 years.*

Maybe during the winter I'll look at this over a longer arc of time. For now, though, we can definitively say quality starts are the best they've ever been since the Diamondbacks and Rays joined the majors.

Yet, paradoxically, they're down.

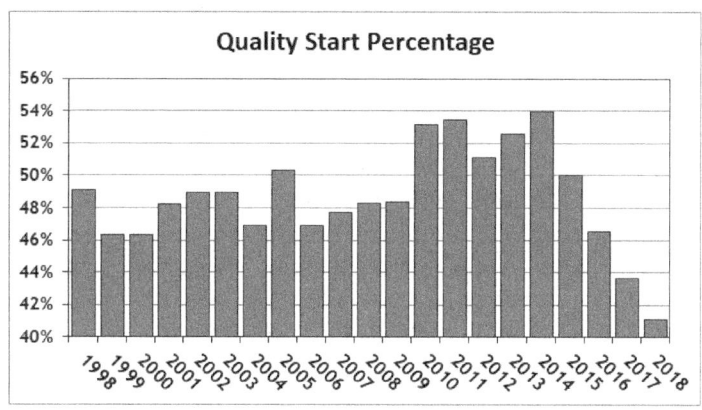

This graph covers only the 30-team era. In my article last week, though, I looked at the years 1908-2018. The result was the same. The 41 percent of starts in 2018 that were quality starts are an all-time low, well below the runners-up: 1930's 43 percent (the year teams scored an all-time record 5.55 runs per game) and last year's 44 percent.

The normal explanation for a dip in quality start percentage is an increase in scoring. When teams score a lot of runs, it's harder for starting pitchers to last six or more innings and limit opponents to three earned runs. From 1998 to 2014, the correlation between runs scored per game and the percentage of starts that were quality starts was -0.94. That means there was an extremely close relationship: More runs, fewer quality starts. Too small a sample? Go back to the start of the Expansion Era, 1961, and the relationship is even more negative, a -0.95 correlation, though 2014.

But that's broken down over the past four years:

- 2015: Runs per game increased from 4.07 to 4.25, quality start percentage decreased from 54.0 to 50.1. Yes, that's a negative relationship, but the regression model would predict a decline of 1.5 percentage points. We got 3.9 instead.
- 2016: Runs per game increased from 4.25 to 4.48, quality start percentage decreased from 50.1 to 46.6. Past experience would suggest a decline of just 1.8 percentage points. We got 3.4.
- 2017: Runs per game increased from 4.48 to 4.65, quality start percentage decreased from 46.6 to 43.6. Again, the direction's right, but the magnitude isn't. Using the relationship from 1998 to 2014, that increase in scoring should've reduced quality starts by 1.3 percentage points, not 2.9.
- 2018: Runs per game declined from 4.65 to 4.45. That should've resulted in the quality start percentage moving in the other direction, rising 1.6 points. It didn't. It fell 2.6 points, as noted, to an all-time low.

Granted, we're talking about just four years here. Maybe they're outliers. But I don't think they are. Quality starts, as noted, are as good or better than ever. But they're rarer than ever as well. And I think I know why.

To get a quality start, you need to allow three or fewer earned and pitch at least six innings. That's 18 outs. Here's a graph showing the number of starting pitchers who limited their opponents to three or fewer earned runs but got pulled after pitching at least five innings but fewer than six:

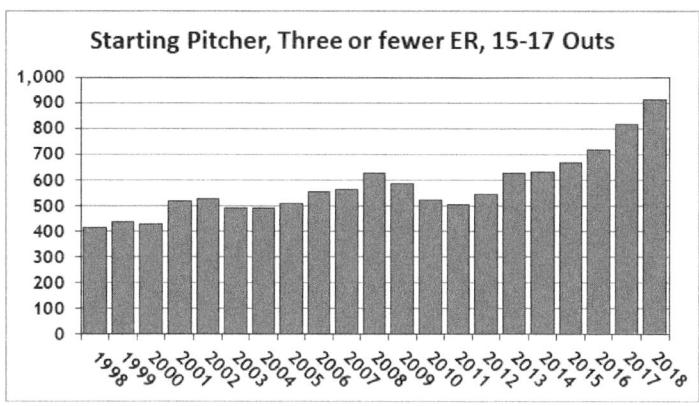

A pitcher getting 15 outs pitched five innings. A pitcher getting 16 outs pitched 5 1/3. A pitcher getting 17 outs pitched 5 2/3. More than ever before, pitchers are being removed from games in which they are within 1-3 outs of a quality start, falling just short of the six-inning finish line. Widespread acknowledgement of the times-through-the-order penalty and a flotilla of available bullpen arms is making the quality start simultaneously both more excellent and more rare.

Which is ironic, given that we saw a new post-war quality start record this season:

Rank	Pitcher	Season	Consecutive QS
1	Jacob deGrom	2018	24
2	Bob Gibson	1968	22
-	Chris Carpenter	2005	22
4	Johan Santana	2004	21
5	Luis Tiant	1968	20
-	Mike Scott	1986	20
-	Jake Arrieta	2015	20
8	Robin Roberts	1952	19
-	Tom Seaver	1973	19
-	Jack Morris	1983	19
-	Greg Maddux	1998	19
-	Josh Johnson	2010	19
-	Jon Lester	2014	19

While there have been longer streaks spread over multiple seasons, no pitcher since World War II threw more consecutive quality starts in one year than Jacob deGrom this year. The fact that he did in a year in which quality starts were the rarest they've ever been adds to the accomplishment.

—*Rob Mains is an author of Baseball Prospectus.*

Heads-Up Hacking—The First Pitch

Matthew Trueblood

Batters fell behind in a higher percentage of all plate appearances in 2018 than in any previous season for which we have pitch-by-pitch data. That kind of granular information goes back only to 1988, but we might safely assume (given all we know about baseball as it had been before that, and as it has been in the years since) that batters have *never* fallen behind at a higher rate than they did last season.

Through the 1990s, the percentage of all plate appearances that began 0-1 hovered in the high 30s and low 40s. In the 2000s, it rose steadily but slowly, through the mid-40s. In 2018, 49.8 percent of all trips to the plate began 0-1. That, as much as anything, captures in microcosm the nature of hitting in MLB today.

A countdown clock toward strike three begins ticking almost the moment a batter takes his place in the box. The league's adjusted OPS+ on the first pitch was higher in 2018 than ever before, and that has been true in most of the last 10 seasons. Batters hit .264/.289/.442 in all plate appearances in which they swung at the first pitch last season, and .241/.330/.395 in all plate appearances in which they took that first offering.

The percentage differences in batting average and isolated power there favor swinging at the first pitch by more than in any season since 1988, while the difference in on-base percentage favors taking by more than ever. If you want to get on base at a decent clip, it's a good idea to be patient, but you run the risk of missing the only chances you'll get to produce power.

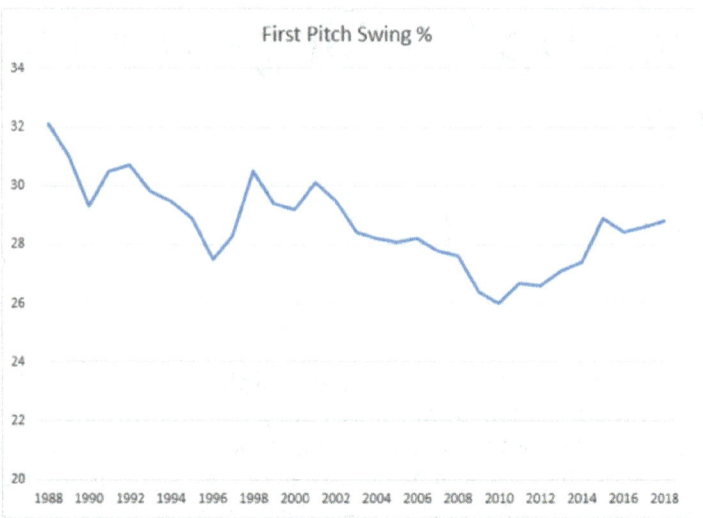

The league swung at the first pitch 28.8 percent of the time in 2018. With the isolated exception of 2015, that's the highest that number has climbed since 2002, but it might not be high enough. With the help of BP research maven Rob McQuown, I looked at the aggregate Called Strike Probability (CSProb) on the first pitch for each season since 2008, when the implementation of PITCHf/x first made measuring that possible. It's risen sharply during that period.

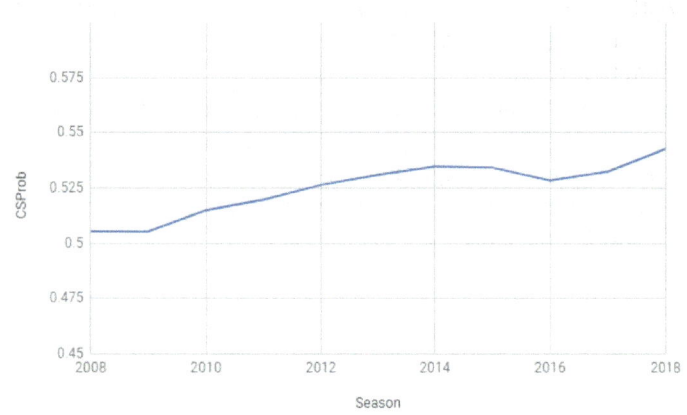

Called Strike Probability, First Pitch of PA (2008-2018)

Called Strike Probability is exactly what it sounds like: a pitch with a given CSProb has roughly that chance of being called a strike, if not swung at. In 2018, a batter who took 100 first pitches from a random sampling of the league's pitchers might expect to fall behind 54 or 55 times—up from 50 or 51 times in 2008. Almost regardless of pitch type (and, notably, especially in the case of fastballs), the first pitch tends to have more of the zone right now than ever before.

Pitchers are better at throwing strikes. They have better stuff, and believe more in their ability to miss bats within the zone. Perhaps most importantly, they know that batters are looking for one thing on the first pitch: a fastball. If they don't get it, they're likely to take the pitch. Check out how the use of sinkers and four-seamers on the first pitch has changed in a decade:

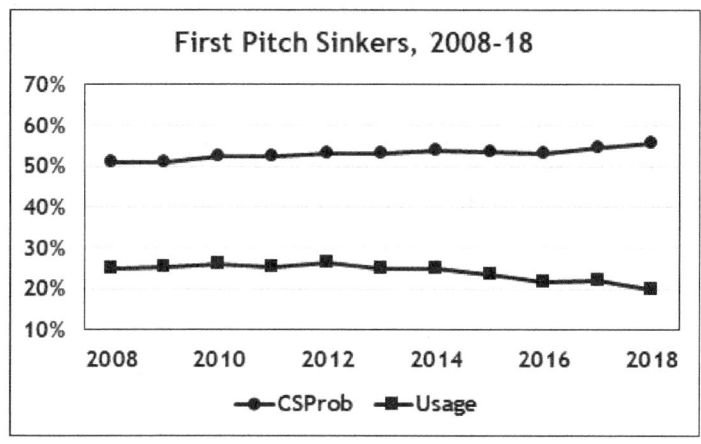

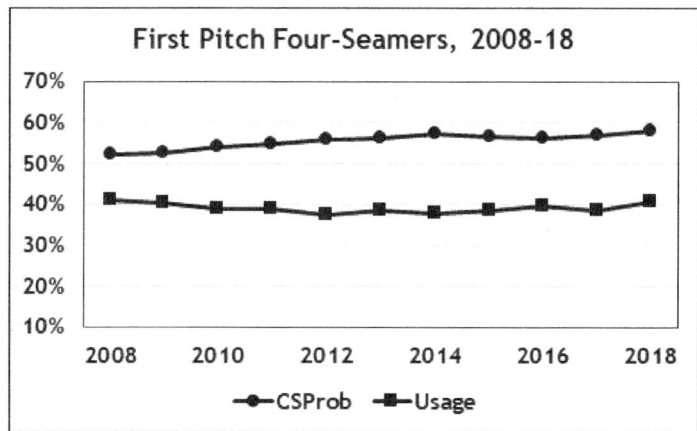

The sinker is losing its place in baseball, but the rate at which pitchers have thrown it on the first pitch hasn't dropped any faster than its usage rate in other counts. Pitchers have actually gone to their four-seamer *more* often to open counts, in the last few years, after a dip in the 2012-2015 period. What's really changed, though, and what shows up in both charts above, is that pitchers are catching more of the zone with first-pitch fastballs than they were a decade ago, or a half-decade ago. They're attacking right away, even with the pitch they know batters are expecting. The message is pretty clear: batters are being too passive.

Sliders, curves, and changeups each have more of the zone when thrown on the first pitch than they did several years ago, too, though the effect is less pronounced. Pitchers have seen the numbers; they know batters are doing better on the first pitch itself. They still feel safe throwing more and better strikes than ever before, figuring they'll come out ahead as long as they keep getting ahead to open each battle.

The Moneyball revolution brought an increased league-wide focus on OBP, which resulted in a de facto mandate to take a more patient tack at the plate. It worked very well for a while, as batters with poor plate discipline were compelled to either adjust or be expelled from the league, and pitchers with poor control were slowly weeded out.

However, concurrent with that revolution, and spurred by it in some ways, was the evolution of the pitching paradigm that now dominates the game. As batters ratcheted up their focus on inflating pitch counts and working walks, pitchers honed theirs on throwing strikes and missing bats. The league's understanding of what makes a good pitcher improved at least as much, from the mid-1990s through the mid-2000s, as its understanding of what makes a good hitter. As amphetamines and other performance-enhancing drugs were phased mostly out of the game, and as PITCHf/x broke onto the scene, individuals and teams learned how to exploit the evolved approaches of even the smartest hitters.

The ability to avoid making outs is still the most valuable one in baseball, but the magnitude of its eclipse of slugging is smaller than ever. To a greater extent than power, on-base skills derive their value from chaining—from the on-base skill levels of the players on either side of a given individual. Eleven years ago, when the housing crisis hit, people learned the hard way that the value of their homes depended a good deal on the values of their neighbors' homes. The same wasn't true, though, of their cars. So it is now, with OBP and SLG.

The global OBP in 2018 was .318. The only seasons since the Dead Ball Era in which the league got on base at a worse clip were 2013-2015, 1988, 1971-1972, and 1963-1968. This is all happening despite the aforementioned evolution of the science of hitting. It's happening despite a shift in approach and focus, one that would steer OBP ever higher, if only it were working.

Instead, it's sitting at a low ebb, and while it does so, even guys who get on base often are a little less helpful than they were 10 years ago—or 20, or 40, or 60, or 70, or 80, or 90. They're less helpful, that is, because unless there happen to be three or four other guys in the lineup who get on just as regularly, their contribution is merely to forestall the inevitable. Runs happen, increasingly, when a sudden bang happens, and that means attacking early in the count—because pitchers are sure as hell doing that.

In a league making contact on barely 75 percent of its swings, and a league in which an increasing number of pitchers can throw multiple off-speed pitches for strikes in any count, the only way to consistently generate offense is going to be aggressive. This isn't necessarily true for individuals, like Mookie Betts and Jose Ramirez, who make a lot of contact and have excellent plate discipline, and whose power comes from such natural quickness in a short stroke. Most players have to make tradeoffs, though, whether it be lowering their contact rate or raising their chase rate, in order to consistently make the quality of contact necessary to survive in today's game.

Highest %	Lowest %
Javier Baez – 48.3	Joe Mauer – 4.6
Freddie Freeman – 47.1	Mookie Betts – 9.7
Ozzie Albies – 46.3	Brett Gardner – 10.7
Jose Altuve – 44.2	Jose Ramirez – 12.0
Nick Castellanos – 44.1	Jason Kipnis – 13.8
Joey Gallo – 42.3	Jesus Aguilar – 14.5
Corey Dickerson – 40.9	Xander Bogaerts – 15.8
Salvador Perez – 40.8	Brian Dozier – 16.3
Eddie Rosario – 40.7	Mike Trout – 17.6
Nick Ahmed – 40.4	Yasmani Grandal – 17.6

Top 10 and Bottom 10 Hitters, First-Pitch Swing Rate (2018)

The question isn't which of these lists one prefers, but what they each convey, qualitatively, about the cat-and-mouse game of early-count hitting. Those top five on the left, especially, drive home the fact that for most players, getting aggressive early in the count is now key to keeping strikeout rate down and hitting for power.

For now, the message is: pitchers are coming right after batters with the nastiest stuff they've ever had. Batters had better stop giving away strike one and force hurlers to adjust, or the global OBP crisis is only going to get worse.

—*Matthew Trueblood is an author of Baseball Prospectus.*

A Hymn for the Index Stat

Patrick Dubuque

We survived without computers. I know this, because I remember the day when my dad hooked up his brand-new Atari 400 computer to the back of our 12-inch Magnavox television, and the perfect blue of the memo pad lit up for the first time. I was born just on the edge of that transitional generation, of learning cursive and balancing checkbooks and just doing math all the time, constant manual arithmetic.

It still amazes me. We learned how to sail ships without computers. We learned how to do calculus. We built towers that didn't fall down, most of the time. We engineered catapults to knock them down anyway. We built a robust system of philosophy called "utilitarianism," founded on the principle that the good of an action is evaluated by summing the effects of that action, which is the kind of formula that would make the world's mainframes crash. The whole foundation of statistics as a field is "here's math you could easily do but would die of old age first."

The fact of the matter is that there is too much math in the world to do. There are too many things changing, and too many things too small to notice, for us to handle. At some point, they become too much for the computers to handle as well, which is why we have chaos theory and undetectable earthquakes, but it's not an even fight. At some point, we fall back on intuition, and given how under-equipped we are, we're forced to bestow that intuition with some sort of supernatural superiority, the "gut feeling," that we can't prove because we can only intuit that our intuition is better.

We're all lousy at intuition, and wonderful at lying to ourselves about it. The honest truth is that computers are far better at intuition than we are, because in order to know what feels "off" you have to know what's "on." In order to do that you have to constantly reassess the average of everything, then re-rank your own experience against it.

Test your own, by comparing these three anonymous lines:

Player	G	HR	AVG	OBP	SLG
Player A	156	38	.259	.342	.535
Player B	154	38	.280	.348	.527
Player C	158	38	.266	.343	.509

These all seem like pretty similar players, right? The second one a touch more batted-ball dependent, the third a little less strong, but all pretty good hitters. And you'd be right, about the latter. Not the former.

Here's the breakdown:

- Player A: 1991 Howard Johnson, 141 DRC+
- Player B: 1996 Dean Palmer, 121 DRC+
- Player C: 2018 Giancarlo Stanton, 114 DRC+

Baseball is fortunate to have escaped the seismic shifts of so many other sports, where the talents and performances of other eras are nearly unrecognizable. (And not just other sports: try to explain the greatness of the movie Duck Soup without adjusting for era.) But they're still there, and they're nearly impossible to account for manually, without having to resort to sweeping generalizations like "steroid era" or juiced-ball era" to throw out entire swathes of production.

This is all to say that we should celebrate the index stat, that simple 100-based scale with such a humble aim: just to give context. It's hard to imagine how we lived without them for so long. Sabermetricians have always tried to make their stats look like other stats: True Average mapped to batting average, FIP molded to look like and compare to ERA. It's easy to understand the motivation—these statistics carry an emotional value in them that is hard to resist, as with the .300 hitter and the 2.00 ERA—but even they fall prey to the same loss of scale as their unadjusted counterparts. If a .300 average means different things in different years, does that hold true for a .300 True Average?

Instead, 100 doesn't say anything, except above average or below. And it does it instantly, for every season in every run environment for any statistic we want it to. We should have more index stats: K%+, so we can stop comparing Mike Clevinger's career 9.46 K/9 to Nolan Ryan's 9.55. HBP%+, so we can note that Ron Hunt was getting plunked when nobody else was getting plunked, as opposed to that imitator Brandon Guyer. Some might note how stale these references are and accuse league-adjustment as a backward-looking drive, and this is true. But we're always looking backward, always comparing the new with the expectations already set. The index stat just forces us to be honest.

There's always resistance to a new statistic, especially one so outwardly simple and so internally complex. We tend to stick with what we know, even in the case of formulas that are supposed to tell us what we know. But if your resistance is that it seems too complicated, too counterintuitive, too "black boxy," I encourage you to consider why you feel that way. Because the real world is infinitely more complicated than baseball, where all the pitches go in one basic direction and the baserunners are only allowed to travel in four directions. Baseball statistics based on mixed methodology are almost impossibly intricate. So are skyscrapers and automobiles. That's why we have computers—to take the guesswork out of them.

—*Patrick Dubuque is an author of Baseball Prospectus.*

Index of Names

Adams, Lane 99
Altherr, Aaron 22
Alvarez, Jose 50
Anderson, Drew 101
Arano, Victor 52
Arrieta, Jake 54
Bohm, Alec 90, 106
Brito, Daniel 99, 112
Butera, Drew 24
Cozens, Dylan 99
Davis, Austin 56
De Los Santos, Enyel 58, 108
Dohy, Kyle 101, 112
Dominguez, Seranthony 60
Duran, Rodolfo 111
Eflin, Zach 62
Eickhoff, Jerad 95
Falter, Bailey 101
Franco, Maikel 26
Gamboa, Arquimedes 99, 110
Garcia, Luis 91, 106
Grullon, Deivi 99, 112
Harper, Bryce 28
Haseley, Adam 92, 107
Hernandez, Cesar 30
Herrera, Odubel 32
Hoskins, Rhys 34
Howard, Spencer 101, 105
Hunter, Tommy 64
Irvin, Cole 96
Kingery, Scott 36

Knapp, Andrew 38
Llovera, Mauricio 101, 112
Marchan, Rafael 99, 111
McCutchen, Andrew 40
Medina, Adonis 97, 104
Moniak, Mickey 93, 108
Morales, Francisco 101, 111
Morgan, Adam 66
Muzziotti, Simon 99
Neris, Hector 68
Neshek, Pat 70
Ngoepe, Gift 99
Nicasio, Juan 72
Nola, Aaron 74
Ortiz, Jhailyn 99, 109
Parkinson, David 101
Pazos, James 76
Petit, Gregorio 99
Pivetta, Nick 78
Plouffe, Trevor 99
Pujols, Jose 94
Quinn, Roman 42
Ramos, Edubray 80
Randolph, Cornelius 99
Realmuto, J.T. 44
Rios, Yacksel 82
Robertson, David 84
Rodriguez, Sean 99
Romero, JoJo 98, 109
Romine, Andrew 99
Rosso, Ramon 101

Philadelphia Phillies 2019

Sanchez, Sixto	103	Velasquez, Vincent	88
Seabold, Connor	101	Walding, Mitch	99
Segura, Jean	46	Williams, Nick	48
Suarez, Ranger	86, 110	Young, Kyle	101

Ballpark diagrams for Baseball Prospectus are created by THIRTY81Project, a design concept offering original ballpark artwork, including the new 'Ballparks of 2019' 11 x 17 color print.

Visit **www.thirty81project.com** for full details.

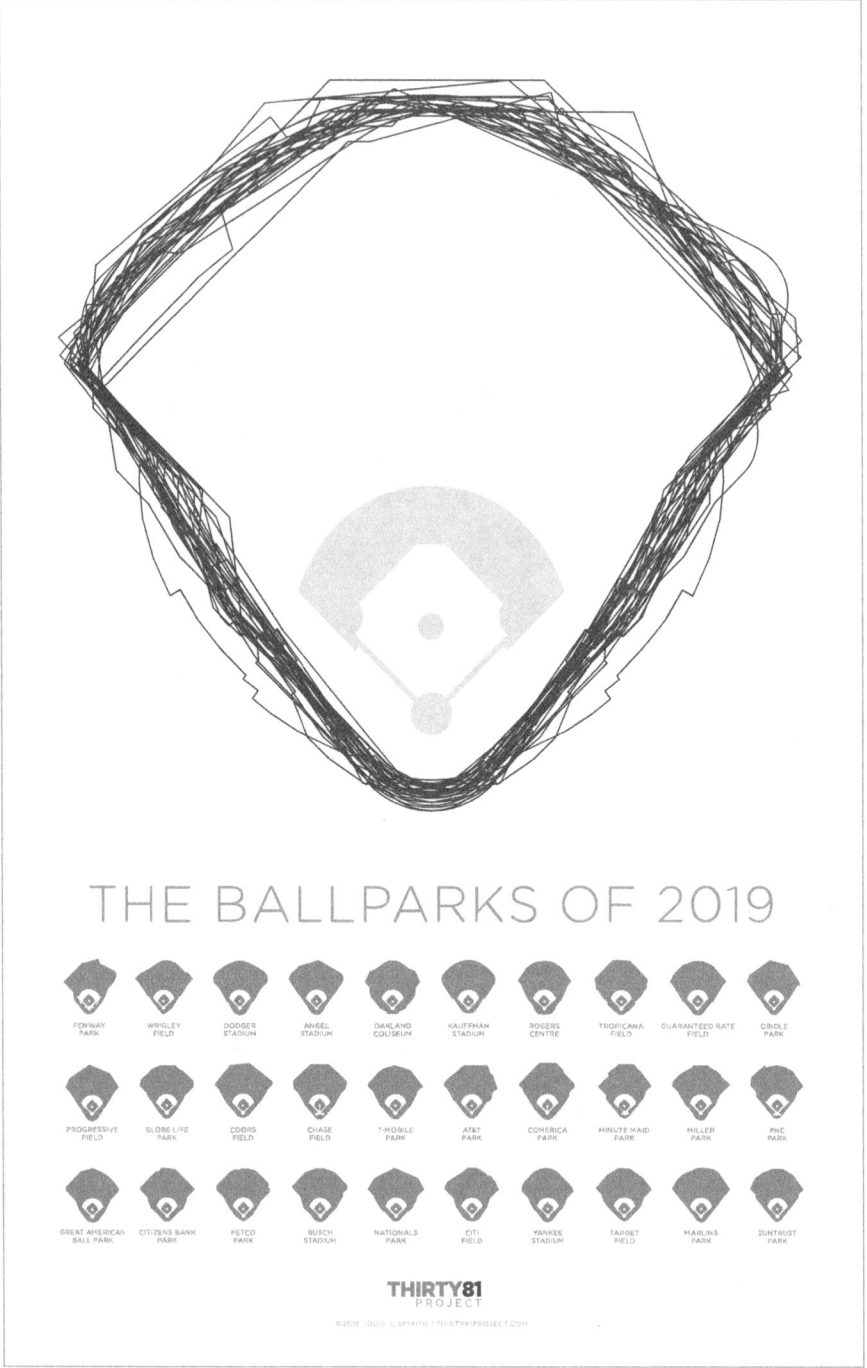